T0161191

SOUL OF THE SAMURAI

THOMAS CLEARY

First published in 2005 by Tuttle Publishing, an imprint of Periplus Editions (HK) Ltd., with editorial offices at 364 Innovation Drive, North Clarendon, VT 05759.

Library of Congress Cataloging-in-Publication Data

Soul of the samurai / [edited] by Thomas Cleary. —1st ed.

  p. cm.

  Includes bibliographical references.

  ISBN 0-8048-3690-6 (hardcover)

  1. Military art and science —Japan—Early works to 1800. 2. Swordplay— Philosophy—Early works to 1800. 3. Martial arts—Religious aspects—Zen Buddhism—Early works to 1800. 4. Zen Buddhism—Doctrines—Early works to 1800. I. Yagyū, Munenori, 1571–1646. Hyōkō kadensho. English. II. Takuan Sōhō, 1573–1645. Fudōchi shinmyōroku. English. III. Takuan Sōhō, 1573–1645. Taiaki. English. IV. Cleary, Thomas F., 1949–

  U101.U668

  796.86'0952-dc22   2005014569

Distributed by

North America, Latin America & Europe

Tuttle Publishing
364 Innovation Drive
North Clarendon, VT 05759-9436
Tel: (802) 773-8930
Fax: (802) 773-6993
info@tuttlepublishing.com
www.tuttlepublishing.com

Japan

Tuttle Publishing
Yaekari Building, 3rd Floor
5-4-12 Ōsaki
Shinagawa-ku
Tokyo 141 0032
Tel: (03) 5437-0171
Fax: (03) 5437-0755
tuttle-sales@gol.com

Asia Pacific

Berkeley Books Pte. Ltd.
130 Joo Seng Road
#06-01/03 Olivine Building
Singapore 368357
Tel: (65) 6280-1330
Fax: (65) 6280-6290
inquiries@periplus.com.sg
www.periplus.com

First edition
09 08 07 06 05   10 9 8 7 6 5 4 3 2 1
Designed by Meg Coughlin Design
Printed in the United States of America

TUTTLE PUBLISHING ® is a registered trademark of Tuttle Publishing.

TABLE OF CONTENTS

Publisher's Note: The original text of the translated works is printed in standard typeface. Dr. Cleary's commentary on the text is printed in italic type.

INTRODUCTION

Martial arts have been associated with esoteric traditions in Asia for many centuries. Military and strategic classics from ancient China show evidence of Taoist influence, while the Japanese warrior code of Bushido, the way of the samurai, was deeply indebted to Zen. The inner traditions of Taoism and Zen imbued the martial arts with ethical outlooks on conflict. Their meditative techniques also trained warriors to be at peace in the midst of battle, fully in command of their faculties, with presence and clarity of mind.

The association of philosophical and religious traditions with martial arts in Asian tradition developed with the emergence of these schools in times of crisis. The early classics of Taoism were compiled in war-torn China, while the development of Zen in medieval Japan was fostered by the ascendant warrior caste. As these historical circumstances produced a wide range of responses in respect to political philosophy, at the same time, mystical undercurrents examined the dynamics of the interface of body, mind, and spirit under conditions of extreme pressure.

Over the centuries, esoteric studies of human interaction led to the articulation of energetics—the workings of energy— at the foundation of strategic science. This is already evident in the military, political, and philosophical classics of China and then highly elaborated in the later syncretic literature of

Taoist yoga and martial arts. The development of Taoist and Buddhist religious militias opposing imperial tyranny in medieval China, moreover, promoted the combination of inner traditions and moral reasoning with martial arts.

Taoism also influenced the development of martial arts in Japan, although it did not take the form of a distinct philosophy or religion in Japan as it did in China. Early Taoism in Japan was amalgamated with so-called Shinto, the Spirit Way, Japan's native shamanistic religion. Shinto, like later Taoism, also absorbed much material from esoteric Tantric Buddhism, which includes arts of destruction in its so-called Sinister Way, or Left-Hand Path.

While the Sinister Way was formally outlawed by the first military government of Japan in the thirteenth century, most of the early Japanese Zen masters were trained in esoteric Buddhism before studying Zen. When martial arts flourished in late medieval Japan under military rule, schools of the sword were associated with esoteric Shinto and Tantrism as well as Zen. Eventually some of the most important Zen masters of later times also incorporated some elements of Shinto and Tantrism into their own teaching.

Indications of the philosophical, ethical, and energetic elements of martial arts are all to be found in the primary Taoist classic *Tao Te Ching*. More technical aspects of the individual use of mind and energy appear in the later Taoist classic *Liezi (Lieh-tzu)* which features the original model of what has come to be known as Zen in the art of archery. Like the *Tao Te Ching* and other Taoist classics, *Liezi* was composed in an era of widespread warfare, when its method of transcending fear was important to ordinary people as well as to warriors.

The *Liezi* was written in a time when Buddhism was being adopted by many new Central Asian kingdoms and making its way into China. While the *Liezi* shows evidence of Buddhist influence, conversely, emerging Chinese Buddhist literature drew on the concepts and vocabulary of Taoism. In this way, the interaction, cross-fertilization, and amalgamation of various elements of Taoism and Buddhism produced new forms of both traditions over the next one thousand years.

When the Mongolian warlord Genghis Khan conquered northern China in the thirteenth century, he learned from his informants that many of the monks of Mount T'ien-t'ai, an ancient center of Buddhism, were skilled in martial arts. He was advised, nevertheless, not to draft them for service in his own armies. The reasoning was that to actually kill people would be disloyalty to the law of Buddhism, and if they were disloyal to the Buddha's law, they couldn't be trusted to be loyal to the Khan's law either.

The Mongol overlords of China subsequently adopted Tantric Buddhism from Central Asia, increasing the influence of Tantrism within China in both Buddhist and Taoist domains. Chinese revolutionaries, on the other hand, used Buddhist and Taoist doctrines and methods to organize peasant revolts against the Mongolian despots and their Chinese successors. By the end of the Ming dynasty in the seventeenth century, the semi-mythical founder of Zen, Bodhidharma, was represented as having transmitted the martial arts then practiced by the monks of Shaolin Temple.

By the time Zen was established in Japan during the thirteenth and fourteenth centuries, the samurai of the higher echelons had set up their own government, overthrowing their allegiance to the aristocracy from which they were descended. Whereas the old aristocracy had patronized the scholarly and ritualistic Tendai and Shingon schools of Buddhism, staffing their oligarchies with relatives and fortifying them with armies of lower-class monks, the shoguns patronized the more austere schools of Zen to create a new cultural model associated with martial rule. Reciprocally, the monks who founded the two main schools of Zen in Japan, Eisai and Dogen, both felt compelled to write essays for their samurai rulers on the advantages of Zen for protection of the state.

The first shogunate declined and collapsed after fleets from Mongol-ruled China tried to invade Japan in the late thirteenth century. In the feudal system of the samurai, outstanding military service had normally been rewarded by land grants; now, however, lack of available lands to compensate all those who defended Japan against the Mongol invasions undermined the standing of the shogun. The resulting unrest eventually culminated in the overthrow and replacement of the shogun by a different warrior clan. This new military government relocated to urban Kyoto, the center of the imperial organization and the old aristocracy, where Zen schools continued to teach professional warriors the genteel arts and social studies imported from China to civilize and refine them for their new roles.

The secular concerns of the leading Zen schools during this era came to overshadow their spiritual contributions, leading to a growing discontent with the character and quality of monastic hierarchy and an increasing outreach of individual Zen masters to the common people. While a large body of secular poetry from official Zen establishments of this era was preserved, it is considered to have no value for spiritual purposes. The practicing schools of Zen, scattered throughout city and country, also declined notoriously in quality. The most outstanding master of the time, the folk hero Ikkyu, is known for his criticism of official Zen schools; celebrating his love for women in erotic poetry, he also wrote that sincere seekers in those days were all abandoning the monasteries.

Ensconced in Kyoto and immersed in the effort to model itself on the old aristocracy, the second shogunate lost effective control of the complex network of feudal alliances that had upheld its precarious power. The fabric of society unraveled in many parts of Japan as samurai in service struggled with their overlords and independents sought to establish themselves. The phenomenon known in Japanese as *ge-koku-jo,* "lower overcoming higher," gave birth to the so-called *Sengoku Jidai,* or Era of the Warring States, in which military prowess was the primary measure of men.

The situation of the samurai changed radically in the sixteenth century with the introduction of firearms from Europe. While the Japanese longbow had more range and accuracy than an unrifled musket, the power of the cannon created a revolution in castle building. Seeing his opportunity, the warlord Oda Nobunaga (1534–1582) converted to Christianity and ordered all his vassals to do likewise, the better to cultivate their connection to European arms dealers. Turning against the redoubtable secular power of organized Buddhism, he razed the ancient stronghold of the Tendai school on Mount Hiei outside Kyoto. By the time of his assassination at the hands of one of his generals, Nobunaga had nearly unified Japan.

Oda Nobunaga's successor, the dictator Toyotomi Hideyoshi, continued Nobunaga's support of Christianity and persecution of Buddhism while warring to complete his unification of Japan. Once he had conquered or compromised rivals, disarmed the farmers, and gained a measure of domestic security, Hideyoshi then turned on the Christian missions, perceiving alien political purpose in them. Apparently intoxicated by lust for power, referred to negatively in martial arts terminology as *blood-energy,* Hideyoshi attempted to invade China through Korea, ruining the opportunity for a Pacific alliance against the growing aggression of Western powers.

Hideyoshi's successor, Tokugawa Ieyasu, completed the unification of Japan and established himself as the first shogun of a new *bakufu,* military government, formally founded in 1603. This regime lasted until 1867, its lengthy reign known to historians as the Tokugawa era, after the family name of the lineage of shoguns, or as the Edo period, after its government seat in the new city of Edo, modern Tokyo.

As part of the organizational scheme of the new military government, the samurai were removed from the land and concentrated in administrative centers, where they might serve as bureaucrats and security forces, and where they might also be more conveniently kept under surveillance themselves. Samurai in private life often became schoolteachers or physicians, while many who continued the military traditions of hereditary warriors ran schools of swordsmanship and other martial arts for the sons of samurai. Samurai of lesser ranks or junior descent commonly entered religious orders and became Zen monks.

The incorporation of Zen into martial arts in Japan was technically based on the mental foundation of Zen meditation as applied to confrontation and combat, while socially and culturally fostered by the concentration of these interests in the same class, clans, and families. The collaboration of experts in these fields is perhaps nowhere more marked than in the seventeenth-century work of the sword master Yagyu Munenori and his Zen teacher Takuan Soho, each tutor to the shogun in their respective domains.

This book presents the teachings of Yagyu and Takuan on swordsmanship and Zen.

Yagyu was both sword teacher and chief of the secret police for the shogun, while Takuan was a *kokushi,* national teacher, Zen mentor of the emperor. The Zen master Takuan's instruction and influence are evident in the sword master Yagyu's work on Zen swordsmanship, *Martial Arts: The Book of Family Traditions.* Some of the Zen master's original input, moreover, is to be found in his writings for the sword master, *The Inscrutable Subtlety of Immovable Wisdom*, a series of explanations of Zen topics in Japanese, and T*ai-A Ki: Notes on the Peerless Sword*, a cryptic treatise in *Kanbun* (Chinese) on the Zen sword, with Takuan's own elucidation in Japanese.

Soul of the Samurai presents contemporary translations of these three classics of Zen Bushido.

MARTIAL ARTS:
THE BOOK OF FAMILY TRADITIONS

By Yagyu Munenori (1571–1646)

Including:

Book 1: The Killing Sword

Book 2: The Life-Giving Sword

Book 3: No Sword

Book I

THE KILLING SWORD

Preface

There is something said of old: "Weapons are instruments of ill omen; it is the Way of Nature to dislike them. To use them only when it is unavoidable is the Way of Nature."

What does this saying mean? Bow and arrow, sword, halberd—these are called weapons; this saying means these are instruments of misfortune and ill omen.

The reason that weapons are instruments of ill omen is that the Way of Nature is the Tao that gives life to beings, so to take to killing instead is indeed an instrumentality of ill omen. Thus the saying has it that what contradicts the Way of Nature it dislikes.

The old saying cited by the samurai here is paraphrased from the Taoist classic Tao Te Ching: *"Fine weapons are instruments of ill omen; people may despise them, so those who have attained the Tao do not dwell with them. . . . Weapons, being instruments of ill omen, are not the tools of the cultured, who use them only when unavoidable." The same text also says, "Those who assist human leaders with the Tao do not coerce the world with weapons, for these things are apt to backfire."*

Nevertheless, it also says that to use weapons to kill people when it is unavoidable is also the Way of Nature. What does this mean? Though flowers blossom and greenery grows in the spring breeze, when the autumn frost comes, the leaves always drop and the trees wither. This is the judgment of Nature.

This is when there is reason to strike something down when it's done. People may take advantage of events to do evil, but when that evil is done, it is attacked. That is why it is said that using weapons is also the Way of Nature.

The Master of the Hidden Storehouse, *another Taoist text, presents a necessity-based defense and deterrence rationale of weaponry and warfare, in contradistinction to the impractical idealism of ideological pacifism:*

"There are those who have died from ingesting drugs, but it is wrong to wish to ban all medicines because of that. There are those who have died sailing in boats, but it is wrong to forbid the use of boats because of that. There are those who have lost countries by waging war, but it is wrong to wish to ban all warfare on that account.

"It is not possible to dispense with warfare, any more than it is possible to dispense with water and fire. Properly used, it produces good fortune; improperly used, it produces calamity. For this reason, anger and punishment cannot be eliminated in the home, criminal and civil sanctions cannot be eliminated in the nation, and punitive expeditions cannot be done away with in the world."

It may happen that a multitude of people suffer because of the evil of one person. In such a case, by killing one man a multitude of people are given life. Would this not be a true example of the saying that "the sword that kills is that sword that gives life?"

The Master of the Hidden Storehouse says, "Ancient sage kings had militias of justice; they did not do away with warfare. When warfare is truly just, it is used to eliminate brutal rulers and rescue those in misery."

The Buddhist Scripture of the Great Demise says, "If bodhisattvas practice conventional tolerance and don't deter evildoing people, allowing them to perpetuate and extend their evil so as to ruin legitimate order, these bodhisattvas are devils, not bodhisattvas."

"The sword that kills is the sword that gives life" is a Zen expression. In Zen literature it is never employed as Yagyu uses it here, to refer to actual killing and warfare. In Zen it refers to the mystic initiation known as the Great Death, by which the limitations of artificial conditioning are transcended. The experience of life after the Great Death is richer than before, so it is said that the sword that kills is the sword that gives life.

There is a science to the use of weaponry. If you try to kill someone without knowing the science, you will probably be killed yourself.

Sun-tzu, the Chinese master of military strategy, wrote, "Those who are not versed in the disadvantages of the use of arms cannot really know the advantages of the use of arms."

In matters of martial arts, the martial art involved in facing off with another using two swords has but one winner and one loser. This is very small-scale martial art; what is won or lost by victory or defeat is little. But when the whole land wins on one individual's victory, or the whole land loses on one individual's defeat, this is martial art on a large scale.

The one individual is the commander; the whole land is the military forces. The forces are the hands and feet of the commander. To operate the forces skillfully means to get the hands and feet of the commander to work well. If the forces do not function, that means the hands and feet of the commander do not work.

Just as one faces off with two swords, exercising the great function of the great potential, using one's hands and feet skillfully to prevail, in the same way, the commander's art of war, properly speaking, is to successfully employ all forces and skillfully exercise strategic tactics to win in battle.

In The Art of War, *Sun-tzu wrote, "Those skilled in military operations achieve cooperation in a group, such that directing the group is like directing a single individual who has no other choice." In a commentary on Sun-tzu, the military theorist Chia Lin wrote, "If leaders can be humane and just, sharing both advantages and problems of the people, then troops will be loyal, identifying with the interests of the leadership of their own accord."*

The Master of the Hidden Storehouse *says, "What determines victory or defeat should not be sought elsewhere but in human feelings. Human feelings imply desire for life and repugnance for death, desire for glory and dislike of disgrace. When there is but one way to determine whether they die or live, to earn ignominy or glory, then the soldiers of the military forces can be made to be of one mind."*

While it is a matter of course, moreover, to go out onto the battlefield to determine victory and defeat when two combat formations are pitched against one another, a commander pitches two combat formations in his chest to try mentally leading a great army into battle—this is the art of war in the mind.

The importance placed on the mental art of war implies that simple force is not adequate to ensure victory in the absence of successful strategy directing its employ. The success of strategic deployment is also a key factor in maintaining the loyalty and morale of the troops, demonstrating both reliability in tactical command and consideration for the welfare of the soldiers.

Not to forget about disturbance when times are peaceful—this is an art of war. To see the dynamic of the state and discern when there is likely to be disruption, and to heal the disturbance before it happens—this is also an art of war.

Sun-tzu wrote in The Art of War, *"The superior martial artist strikes while schemes are being laid." Tu Yu cited an emperor-general to illustrate Sun-tzu's principle: "Those who are skilled at eliminating trouble are those who deal with it before it happens. Those who are skilled at prevailing over opponents are those who win before there is formation."*

Once there is peace, to give consideration to the selection of governors and administrators of all regions, and to national security, is also a martial art. When governors, administrators, magistrates, and local lords oppress the common people in pursuit of personal profit, this above all is the beginning of the end for a nation. Observing the situation carefully, planning so as to prevent the nation from perishing through the self-seeking of those governors, administrators, magistrates, and local lords, is like watching an opponent in a duel to see if he has anything up his sleeve. It is imperative to observe with utmost attention; this is what makes martial art a matter of such great moment.

The Indian strategist Kautilya, advisor to the founder of the great Maurya Dynasty in the fourth century BCE, wrote in his classic Art of Wealth, *"An embedded thorn, a loose tooth, and a bad administrator—these are best rooted out." He also wrote, by way of warning, "Even the course of birds flying in the sky may be discerned, but not so the course taken by appointees who conceal their true condition."*

There are also treacherous people surrounding rulers, people who pretend to be upright when in the presence of superiors yet look on subordinates with a glare in their eyes. Unless they are bribed, they represent the good as bad, so the innocent suffer while the guilty gloat. To perceive the beginning of this is even more urgent than to notice a secret plot.

Yagyu Munenori, author of this work, headed the shogun's secret service, overseeing the direct vassals. His appointment is dated to the year he finished this book on martial arts, but by the time of this writing he was already tutor to the shogun, and his observation on corruption in government reflects a professional as well as a personal concern. Because of the strict hierarchical nature of Japanese feudal organization, compromise in higher circles created particular problems for a fiefdom, endangering the integrity of the entire organization.

Yagyu's Zen mentor, Takuan, was not so ready to blame this all on interlopers but looked to the role of the leadership: "They say that if you want to know people's merits and faults, you can tell by the help they employ and the friends with whom they associate. If the leader is good, the members of the cabinet are all good people. If the leader is not right, his cabinet and friends are all wrong. Then they disregard the populace and look down on other countries."

The country is the ruler's country; the people are the ruler's people. Those who serve the ruler directly are as much subjects of the ruler as those who serve indirectly. How far apart are they? They are like hands and feet in the service of the ruler. Are the feet different from the hands because they are farther away? Since they both feel pain and discomfort the same, which can be called nearer, which further away? But if those close to the ruler bleed those far away and cause the innocent to suffer, the people will resent the ruler even though he is honest.

This passage illustrates the responsibility of every member of an organization in maintaining its overall integrity, while showing how a top-down model of government places a particular burden of responsibility on the circle surrounding the leadership. The absolutist model employed here thus demonstrates an essential flaw of feudalism. In the context of medieval Japan, the idea that the ruler is the owner of the nation and people probably derived from the deification of the emperor. It has no Zen or Buddhist content or counterpart and provides the pattern for all manner of corruption.

The systemic flaw in this model of government, perpetuated for centuries, created the expectation system that enabled fascism and militarism to resume control of Japan in modern times and even embark on imperialism. For someone in Yagyu's position, nonetheless, absolutism is the default model, and here the sword master simply alludes to the fact that an organization is like an organism whose various parts all contribute to the operation of the whole, and the higher the position the more powerful the effects of individual actions on the entirety.

There are only a few people close to a ruler, perhaps five or ten. The majority of people are remote from rulers. When many people resent their ruler, they will express their feelings. Now, when the minority close to the ruler have been after their own interests all along instead of acting in consideration of the ruler, and so serve in such a way that the people resent the ruler, then when the time comes those close to the ruler will be the first to set upon him. Then who will think of the ruler? This is the doing of those close to the ruler, not the personal fault of the ruler. The potential for this ought to be clearly perceived, and those distant from the rulership should not be excluded from its benefits. Since this is a matter of perceiving the potential accurately at the outset, it too is a martial art.

> *Here again Yagyu takes the side of the ruler versus corrupt associates, in contrast to his Zen teacher Takuan's observation that the associations of the leadership are themselves indications of its ethical quality. In practical terms, vertical absolutism isolated the individuals at the apex of the pyramid, creating the opportunity for conspiring cabinet members to deceive the ruler while manipulating delegated authority. When the ruler is kept ignorant while the cabinet exploits its privileges, the people may become rebellious without the ruler knowing why.*

In social and professional relationships, moreover, the attitude is the same as that of a warrior, even when there is no discord, in that you act as you see situations develop. The mindfulness to watch the dynamic of situations even in a group is a martial art.

> *The defining element of the art of war in this sense is not conflict or armament, but deliberate application of situational strategy in all manner of interactions.*

If you do not see the dynamic of a situation, you may remain too long in company where you should not be, and thus get into trouble for no reason. When people say things without observing others' states of mind, thus getting into arguments and even forfeiting their lives as a result, this all hinges on seeing or not seeing the dynamic of a situation and the states of the people involved.

In feudal organizations, personal relationships were critical elements of social and political order, so their manners and customs of interaction were highly ritualized. Among the samurai, cultivated class and clan pride could create problems and perils even in social situations; elaborately regulated formalities of speech and conduct were used to insulate emotions. The stiffness that this produced was softened to some extent by the custom of drinking parties, as is indeed still the case today, but even in such situations excessive loosening of the tongue could lead to disaster.

Even to furnish a room so that everything is in the right place is to see the dynamic of a situation. Thus it involves something of the mindfulness of the warrior's art.

The art of furnishing a room for specific psychological and aesthetic effects was a specialty of the masters of the tea ceremony, cha-no-yu, *which was allegedly imported from China by medieval Zen masters and adapted to Japanese culture as a means of mellowing the spirit of the samurai, who were engaged in class warfare against the old aristocracy.*

Indeed, although the phenomena may differ, the principle is the same. Therefore it can also be applied accurately to the affairs of state.

It is a Taoist convention to draw analogies between the governance of the individual body and the governance of groups, both military and political. Therefore the principles of self-discipline and self-mastery are applied to the principles of leadership and authority. Here the principle is adaptation to situations on the basis of objective perception, whether in the context of the everyday life of the individual, or in a strategic approach to state organization, operation, and planning.

The relationship between principle and phenomena is also emphasized in Zen Buddhism. The experience of satori, *or awakening, is referred to as the entry into principle, or noumenon, and the obliteration of the artificial inhibitions of intellect this produces gives the impression of mastery. There are many examples of people who have evinced extraordinary capabilities after experiencing satori, such as the ability to master an art without being taught, but there is considerable individual and conditional difference in this, and the confusion of awakening with enlightenment has always been an issue in Zen.*

The tenth-century Chinese Zen master Fayan (885–958) wrote on this problem in a seminal treatise on critical evaluation of Zen schools: "The schools of the enlightened ones always include both principle and fact. Facts are established on the basis of principle, while principle is revealed by means of facts. Principles and facts complement one another like eyes and feet. If you have facts without principle, you get stuck in the mud and cannot get through. If you have principle without facts, you will be vague and without resort. If you want them to be nondual, it is best that they be merged completely."

There is a Zen saying that "principle is realized all at once, while things are worked out gradually." In samurai Zen, the main problem produced by confusion of realization in principle and in fact is the notion that it is only necessary to stop thinking and to react automatically to be in accord with principle in fact. The result is an unconscious amorality that can be manipulated externally, unaware of its aberrations.

To think of the art of war only as killing people is biased. It is not for killing people, it is for killing evil. It is a strategy to give life to many people by killing the evil of one person.

The idea that killing one malicious person will save many oppressed people comes from the vertical model of authoritarian leadership, where the loyalty of subordinates is to the person in the position of authority, not to an abstract code of law or morality. Even so, the definition of just warfare as a means of eliminating oppression can be applied without limitation of social or political system, so long as good and evil are understood in terms of human welfare rather than abstract political orthodoxy. The Master of the Hidden Storehouse *says, "When warfare is truly just, it is used to eliminate brutal rulers and rescue those in misery."*

What is written in these three scrolls is a book that is not to go outside the house. Even so, that does not mean the Way is secret. Secrecy is for the sake of conveying knowledge. If no knowledge is conveyed, that is the same as if there were no book. Let my descendants consider this carefully.

The idea of secret transmission became prominent in both Zen and Bushido during the last feudal age, when the overt activities of monks and samurai were strictly regulated by governmental regulations. In the Rinzai sect of Zen, secrecy surrounding the koan became paramount, while in the Soto sect of Zen a similar occultism shrouded ritual enactment of lineage transmission. In the realm of Bushido both of these forms of esoterism were emulated in the teaching of supposedly secret sword techniques and the organization of martial arts schools in familial and pseudo-familial lineages.

While the secretive nature of Zen and martial arts may have been intensified by political conditions in the fractious world of feudal Japan, the origin of secrecy in esoteric teaching derived from the need to select suitable candidates and to protect society from misuse of knowledge. That is why it is sometimes said that there is no secret, or that the secret is in yourself, whereas it may also be insisted that the secret is in itself ineffable, so that it cannot be explained to another but only acknowledged by oneself.

The Great Learning

It is said that *The Great Learning* is the gateway to elementary learning. When you go to a house, first you go in through the gate; thus the gate is an indication that you've arrived at the house. Going through this gate, you enter the house and meet the host.

The Great Learning, or Daigaku in Japanese, is a Confucian classic, one of the so-called Four Books in the secular education system of late feudal Japan. One of the famous lines of The Great Learning *cited in Zen teaching is "The Way of Great Learning is in clarifying enlightened virtue." When asked what this means, the Zen master Bunan said, "Clarifying the mind." In Zen terms, this clarification of mind is what the sword master calls entering the house and meeting the host.*

Learning is the gate to attainment of the Way. You get to the Way by going through this gate. Therefore learning is the gate, not the house. When you see the gate, don't take it for the house. The house is inside, past the gate.

Since learning is a gate, when you read books, don't think this is the Way. Books are a gate to get to the Way. Therefore many people remain ignorant of the Way no matter how much they study or how many words they know. Even if you can read fluently according to the commentaries of the ancients, as long as you are ignorant of the principles you cannot make the Way your own.

> *Zen Buddhism emphasizes practical application rather than theoretical disquisition, distinguishing academic or intellectual enterprise from studies conducive to spiritual enlightenment. Study without practice, or reading without understanding, is commonly called "counting the treasures of another without having a penny of one's own." Traditional teachings also take note, however, of the perils of the other extreme, where ignorance is considered bliss and abandonment of formal learning deprives people of information critical to their development.*

Even so, to attain the Way without learning is difficult too. Yet it is impossible to say that someone understands the Way just because he is learned and articulate. There are some people who accord with the Way spontaneously, without learning how.

> *One of the most famous stories of Zen tradition concerns the recognition of the Sixth Grand Master in China in the seventh century, during the era of the founders. The Fifth Grand Master was an eminent monk with hundreds of disciples who were highly*

educated. When the time came to appoint a successor, the Fifth Grand Master announced a kind of contest, in which the composer of the best poem on Zen would become the next Grand Master. Everyone deferred to the chief disciple, a distinguished scholar, but he was trumped by a lay kitchen laborer, an illiterate woodcutter who had what the Zen classics call Teacherless Wisdom.

The Great Learning speaks of consummating knowledge and perfecting things. Consummating knowledge means thoroughly knowing the principles of everything that people in the world know. Perfecting things means that when you thoroughly know the principles of everything, then you know everything and can do everything. When knowledge is consummated, things get done too. When you do not know the principles, nothing at all comes to fruition.

The Four Books were standard curriculum in terakoya, temple elementary schools, conventionally taught by local Zen monks. Many quotations from these Confucian classics are therefore found in the colloquial sayings and vernacular writings of Japanese Zen masters of that era.

For the samurai of highest rank who ran the military government, the political reasons for establishment of neo-Confucianism as standard curriculum were readily found in their interest in social order after the stabilization of the martial regime. For Zen monks, appeal to Confucian classics in the context of knowledge and action could also act as a shield against suspicions that Zen might be relevant to the world. At that time the military government had assumed legal control of the Zen establishments; official policy forbade innovation and encouraged academic scholarship as an occupation among career monks.

It is nevertheless the fact that Zen teaching includes ethical, social, and general humanitarian concerns, and some of the latter-day masters made this clear even under the repressive conditions of feudal absolutism that tried to relegate Zen to esoteric cultism. Zen master Hakuin, who founded a new line of koan study within the Rinzai sect of Zen in the eighteenth century, wrote in these terms of knowledge and action:

"Having reached the nondual sphere of equality of true reality, at this point it is essential to attain clear understanding of the enlightened ones' profound principles of differentiation, and master methods of helping people. Otherwise, even if you have cultivated and realized unobstructed insight, you will remain in the nest of a lesser vehicle after all and be unable to realize omniscience, unhindered knowledge, and the freedom to adapt in any way necessary to help others. You will be unable to enlighten yourself and enlighten others, or reach the ultimate great enlightenment in which awareness and action are completely perfected. For this reason it is essential to conceive an attitude of great compassion and commitment to help all people everywhere."

In all things, uncertainty exists because of not knowing. Being doubtful, those things stay on your mind. When the principle is clarified, nothing stays on your mind. This is called consummating knowledge and perfecting things. Once there is nothing on your mind, everything becomes easy to do.

The Zen master Hakuin wrote, "Observing knowledge is accomplished by successful practice; it is in the realm of cultivation and realization, of attainment by study. This is called knowledge involving effort. Practical knowledge, in contrast, transcends the bounds of practice, realization, and attainment through study. It is beyond the reach of indication and explanation."

For this reason, the practice of all the arts is to clear away what is on your mind. At first you don't know anything, so you don't have any uncertainty in mind. Then when you enter into study, there is something on your mind and you are inhibited by that, so everything becomes hard to do.

When the object of your study leaves your mind entirely, and practice also disappears, then when you perform the art in which you are engaged you accomplish the techniques easily without being inhibited by concern over what you've learned, yet without deviating from what you've learned. This is spontaneous accord with learning, without subjective awareness of doing so. This is how the science of martial art is to be understood.

Hakuin wrote, "Observing knowledge is like the blossoming of the flower of full awakening and practice, while practical knowledge, that is knowledge to do what is to be done, is like the blossom of full awakening and practice dropping away and the actual fruit forming."

To learn all the sword strokes, the physical postures, and the focus of the eyes, to learn all there is to learn and to practice it, is the meaning of consummating knowledge. Then when you have succeeded in learning, when everything you've learned disappears from your conscious mind and you become innocent, this is the meaning of perfecting things.

When you have perfected all sorts of exercises and built up achievement in cultivation of learning and practice, even as your hands, feet, and body act it does not hang on your mind. You are detached from your learning, and yet you do not deviate from your learning. Your action is free whatever you do.

At this time, there's no telling where your mind is — not even the celestial devil, or outsiders either, can spy into your heart. The learning is for the purpose of reaching this state. Once you have learned this successfully, learning disappears.

This is the ultimate sense and the progressive transcendentalism of all the Zen arts. Forgetting learning, relinquishing mind completely, harmonizing without any subjective awareness of it, is the consummation of the Way. This stage is a matter of entering from learning into freedom from learning.

> *Here the sword master is alluding to the stage of accomplishment known in Zen as mindlessness. The image of being inaccessible is a classic Zen motif, taken directly from Zen literature. In Zen psycho-cosmology, the celestial devil stands for the conceptual consciousness. It is called celestial because this devil inhabits the "heaven of command of others' emanations," which symbolizes conceptual manipulation of information of the senses and perceptions.*
>
> *The term "outsiders" in Zen parlance refers to attachments to external objects, including abstract objects such as doctrines, philosophies, or conceptual interpretations of experience in general. In Buddhist terms, the process of getting to this transcendence is called "learning," while the result, competence beyond conceptual manipulation and interpretation, is called "freedom from learning."*

Energy and Will

The mind with a specific inward attitude and intensive concentration of thought is called will. Will being within, what emanates outwardly is called energy.

To give an illustration, the will is like the master of a house, while the energy is like a servant. The will is within, employing energy.

If energy rushes out too much, you will stumble. Make your will restrain your energy so that it does not hurry.

In the context of martial arts, lowering the center of gravity can be called will. Facing off to kill or be killed can be called energy. Lower your center of gravity securely, and don't let your energy become hasty and aggressive.

It is essential to control your energy by means of will, calming down so that your will is not drawn by your energy.

The Chinese strategic classic The Master of Demon Valley *says, "Development of will is for when the energy of mind does not reach the intended object. When you have some desire, your will dwells on it and intends it. Will is a functionary of desire. When you have many desires, then your mind is scattered; when your mind is scattered, then your will deteriorates. When your will deteriorates, then thought does not attain its object."*

From this point of view, the austerity and discipline of the warrior's life is a means of concentration in order to cultivate will. This is not only for self-mastery, but for strategic elusiveness and control of energetic emanation. The same classic says, "When psychological conditions change within, physical manifestations appear outwardly. Therefore it is always necessary to discern what is concealed by way of what is visible." The inscrutability of the master martial artist is precisely for the purpose of making enemies unable to predict their moves.

Appearance and Intention

Appearance and intention are fundamental to the art of war. Appearance and intention mean the strategic use of ploys, the use of deception to gain what is real.

Appearance and intention invariably ensnare people when artfully employed, even if people sense that there is an ulterior intention beyond the overt appearance. When you set up your ploys, opponents fall for them; you win by letting them act on your ruse.

As for those who do not fall for a ploy, when you see they won't fall into one trap, you have another one set. Then even opponents who aren't inveigled wind up being inveigled.

In Buddhism this is called expedient means. Even though the real truth is hidden inside while strategy is employed outwardly, when you are finally led into the true path the pretenses now all become true.

In Shinto there is what is called the mystery of the spirits. The mystery is kept secret in order to foster religious faith. When there is faith, there is charity.

In the warrior's way, this is called strategy. Although strategy is pretense, when the pretense is used to win without hurting people, the pretense turns out true. This is an example of what is called achieving harmonious order by means of its opposite.

The master strategist Sun-tzu wrote in The Art of War, *"To take up a posture or a disposition means to manipulate strategy according to advantage. Warfare is a path of subterfuge. That is why you make a show of incompetence when you are actually competent, you make a show of ineffectiveness when you are in fact effective. When nearby you appear to be distant, when distant you appear to be nearby." In the context of warfare, Yagyu's statement that the purpose of strategic deception is to win without hurting people means that victory by tactical superiority is less costly in lives than victory by sheer force.*

Beating the Grass to Scare the Snakes

There is something in Zen called beating the grass to scare the snakes. To startle or surprise people a little is a device, like hitting at snakes in the grass to scare them.

An unexpected action used as a ploy to startle an opponent is also an appearance concealing an ulterior intention, an art of war. When an opponent is startled and the sense of opposition is distracted, the opponent will experience a gap in reaction time. Even holding up a fan or raising your hand distracts an opponent's attention.

Throwing down your own sword is also an art of war. If you have attained mastery of swordlessness, you will never lack for a sword. The opponent's sword is your sword. This is acting at the vanguard of the moment.

In Zen teaching method, intentional output designed to provoke reaction is called beating the grass to scare the snakes. A Zen master's statement or question, therefore, or an action or gesture, may not be intended to convey a meaning or message in itself, but to bring out the mentality of a student for observation. In martial arts, the analogy is to a feint, a gesture, look, or attitude intended to induce an opponent to act in haste, thus exposing himself to counterattack, or to mistakenly defend the wrong target while leaving the intended target open. Feinting is not only a means of distracting an opponent's attention from the intended target to neutralize defensive maneuvers, it is also a means of eliciting and interpreting the opponent's particular habits and skills.

The art of swordlessness is not a Zen paradox but a reference to resourcefulness. This is discussed in more detail in the third scroll of this work, entitled "No Sword." In a sword fight, swordlessness might involve snatching away an opponent's sword.

This may be done by slipping inside an opponent's swing to hit his lead grip hand with your fist as he tries to strike with his sword. This method adds the momentum of the opponent's movement to the force of your blocking fist; if you can hit the middle of his finger bones, or his hand bones, with the edge of your knuckles, you can break his hand and take his sword. This is why the back of the hand is normally guarded in spite of the fact that the protective material would not stop a sword.

An advanced technique involves slapping the palms directly together on the sword as the opponent slashes, pinning it between the palms so as to arrest the flight of the blade in midair. Then the joined palms are twisted to flip the opponent's sword out of his hand.

Throwing down one's own sword is a means of inducing the opponent to strike, while draining power from the opponent's blow by releasing tension from the fray. This makes it easier to arrest the blade in flight and snatch it away, "making the opponent's sword your sword."

The Vanguard of the Moment

The vanguard of the moment is before the opponent has begun to make a move. This first impulse of movement is the energy held back in the chest. The dynamic of the movement is energy. To observe an opponent's energy carefully and act to counter it in advance of the energy is called the vanguard of the moment.

This effective action is a specialty of Zen, where it is referred to as the Zen dynamic.

The energy that is hidden within and not revealed is called the potential of the moment. It is like a hinge, which is inside the door. To observe the invisible workings hidden inside and act thereupon is called the art of war at the vanguard of the moment.

Expert martial artists can read the kehai, *or energetic emanation, of other people by sensing it with their own bodies. The meaning of the vanguard of the moment is the response to an energetic impulse before it is transmitted into action. Stories of Zen masters awakening students by shocks such as shouting or striking appear paradoxical or irrational on the surface because the underlying element of energy perception is not represented overtly and is only understood through experience. Without precise timing so as to intercept an energetic impulse prior to expression, Zen shock techniques are not effective.*

Aggressive and Passive Modes

The aggressive mode is when you attack intently, slashing with extreme ferocity the instant you face off, aggressively seeking to get in the first blow.

The sense of aggression is the same whether it is in the mind of the opponent or in your own mind.

The passive mode is when you do not attack precipitously but wait for the opponent to make the first move. Being extremely careful should be understood as a passive mode.

The aggressive and passive modes refer to the distinction between attacking and waiting.

> *The aggressive mode of instant unrelenting attack is used to strike while an opponent is still cold and has no momentum. The intent is to overwhelm the opponent all at once, foiling maneuvers before any action can be launched. The passive mode is used to wear out an opponent's energy while conserving one's own, waiting and watching to read the opponent's tactics and find a gap in the opponent's defense.*

Principles of Aggressive and Passive Modes of the Body and the Sword

Looming over your opponent with your body in an aggressive attitude and your sword in a passive attitude, you use your body, feet, or hands to draw out a first move from your opponent, gaining victory by inducing your opponent to take the initiative. Thus your body and feet are in an aggressive mode while your sword is in a passive mode.

The purpose of putting your body and feet in the aggressive mode is to get your opponent to make the first move.

> *The aggressive attitude of the body is adopted to draw a defensive or preemptive maneuver from the opponent, so that a gap in the opponent's defense opens up in the*

act of making a move. The sword hitherto held in a passive mode is then activated to deliver a corresponding counteroffensive, according to the opponent's move.

Aggressive and Passive Modes of Mind and Body

The mind should be in the passive mode, the body in the aggressive mode. Why? If the mind is in the aggressive mode, your steps will be hurried, which is bad; so you should control the mind, keeping it impassive, while using physical aggressiveness to get the opponent to make the first move —thus you gain victory. If your mind is aggressive, you'll lose by trying to kill your opponent at once.

In another sense, it can be understood that the mind is to be in the aggressive mode and the body in the passive mode. The point of this is to cause your mind to work relentlessly, putting the mind in an aggressive mode while keeping your sword passive, to get the adversary to make the first move.

The body can be understood simply to mean the hands that hold the sword. Thus it is said that the mind is aggressive while the body is passive.

Although there are two meanings, ultimately the sense is the same. In any case you win by inducing your opponent to take the initiative.

These concepts can be traced back to Chinese strategic classics of the Era of the Warring State. The Art of War *says, "If you induce others to adopt a form while you remain formless, then you will be concentrated while the enemy will be divided."*

The Master of Demon Valley *says, "Pressuring is up to you; response is up to others. When you use this accord-*

ingly, nothing is impossible. The ancients who were skilled at pressuring were as if fishing in a deep body of water, casting in bait and unfailingly catching fish. This is the meaning of the saying that when directing affairs you succeed day by day yet no one knows, when commanding the military you win day by day yet no one fears."

Things to Learn When Facing an Aggressive Opponent

There are three places to focus the eyes: (1) The Two Stars (the opponent's two hands gripping his sword); (2) Peak and Valley (the bending and extension of the opponent's arms); and (3) When engaged, the Distant Mountains (the opponent's shoulders and chest).

The details of these places to focus the eyes are to be transmitted by word of mouth.

The next two items deal with the sword and the physical posture: (1) The rhythm of the distance, and (2) The position of the body and the sandalwood state of mind.

The next five items are in the body and in the sword; they are impossible to explain in writing, and each one must be learned by dueling: (1) Making the fist into a shield; (2) Making the body unified; (3) Taking an opponent's fist on your shoulder; (4) The sense of extending the rear leg; (5) Adopting the same postures as the adversary.

In any case, the proper state of mind in all five items is to prepare yourself carefully before facing off with an opponent, not allowing yourself to be inattentive; it is essential to make sure that you don't get rattled once the duel begins. If you face off all of a sudden without mental preparation, the moves you have learned will not be forthcoming.

The subtle movements of the hands, arms, and torso of an adversary yield information essential to defense, prediction, and preemption. The conditions for each point of focus are explained in the next segment of Yagyu's text—the adversary's elbows, or the bending and extension of the adversary's arms, when wading in slashing; the adversary's shoulders and chest when exchanging blows; and the adversary's hands at all times.

"The rhythm of the distance" refers to the adjustment of position back and forth to maintain a certain distance until there is an opening in the opponent's defense. This distance may be defined as being just beyond the opponent's reach while keeping the opponent within one's own reach. This skill can be learned from animals.

The sandalwood state of mind is a code term for slashing twice in exactly the same line. This is aimed at concentrating momentum and force on an opening gap. The matter of physical posture is invoked here because the technique of slashing twice in the same line is executed in accordance with the angle from which the attack is launched, necessitating a corresponding structural basis in the stance and geometric harmony in the stroke.

"Making the fist into a shield" refers to blocking a sword blow by stopping the "two stars"—the adversary's hands gripping the sword—with a fist. "Making the body unified" refers to distributing ki—energy—throughout the body evenly, without pooling or concentrating it in any fixed place, so that the whole body is like a single organ of sense. "Taking an opponent's fist on the shoulder" refers to blocking the "two stars" with the shoulder by

moving inside the arc of an oncoming sword blow. "Extending the rear leg" means that the balance of the body weight is on the forward leg, while the rear leg is extended to enable the warrior to get out of range without shifting stance, thereby to be able to come right back with a counterattack. Adopting the same postures as the adversary is a mirroring technique for reading the opponent's energetic state by sensing the specific set of physical tensions in a given posture.

Things to Learn When Facing a Passive Opponent

Regarding the significance of these three items—the Two Stars, Peak and Valley, and the Distant Mountains—when an opponent is firmly entrenched in a passive, waiting mode, you shouldn't take your eyes off the places described in these three expressions.

These points of focus, however, are used for both aggressive and passive modes. These points of focus are essential. When wading in slashing, you focus your eyes on the Peak. When exchanging blows, you should be careful to focus your eyes on the Distant Mountains. As for the Two Stars, you should always keep an eye on them.

The Mental Postures of Three Ways of Feinting

The three ways of feinting are three ways of seeing: sticking, pinning, and studied assault. When you cannot tell what opponents might do, you should use these three feints to feel them out.

The point is to find out adversaries' intentions. When opponents are secured in a passive, waiting mode, you cast these three kinds of impressions for the three ways of seeing, implementing strategic maneuvers to induce adversaries to tip their hands, using this to enable you to gain victory.

This also parallels a corresponding Zen method, where the initial endeavor of a teacher is to induce students to exteriorize subjective states so that they can be observed and treated objectively. The Zen saying "the intent is on the hook" alludes to this method, where the point of a Zen statement or question is not in the overt content per se, but in drawing revealing reactions.

Addressing and Adapting to Changes of Attitude

The sense of this is that when you deliberately convey various attitudes to opponents waiting in a passive mode, their attitudes become manifest. You win by adapting to those attitudes.

This is mental feinting, or in Taoist terms "energetic feinting." In a sword fight, with two minds totally concentrated on an interaction, shifts in tension structure are communicated spontaneously through the medium of mutual concentration. Therefore an adversary can be induced to shift mental posture by a change in psychophysical tension structure, just as an adversary can be induced to act out by an alteration of posture or attitude. Either way, the purpose of feinting is in revealing a characteristic pattern of response, so as to be able to anticipate and outmaneuver an opponent.

Double Looks

When you try various ploys on passive opponents to see what they will do, you see without looking, seeing without appearing to see, constantly attentive, not fixing your eyes on one place alone but shifting your eyes around, seeing in quick glances.

There's a line of poetry that says, "Watching in stolen glances, the dragonfly evades the shrike." Seeing a shrike in a stolen glance, a dragonfly takes to flight. Quickly but surely seeing the actions of opponents in stolen glances, you should work with constant attention.

In farcical Noh drama there is something called the double look. This means to look and see, then shift the eyes to the side. This means not fixing the gaze.

There are both offensive and defensive meanings to avoiding fixation of focus. The offensive purposes are to facilitate feinting with the eyes and to keep alert for impulses to act, or openings in defense, appearing in the adversary's physical posture and energy field. The defensive purposes are to observe every movement and be able to evade an attack before it is launched without being misdirected by a feint and to make the adversary unable to discern where your attention or intention may be at any given moment.

Hit and Be Hit At
The Sense of Winning by Letting Yourself Be Hit At

It is easy to kill someone with a single sword slash; it is hard to be impossible for others to cut down. Even if someone lashes out at you with the intention of cutting you down, carefully note the margin of safety where you are out of range, and let yourself be hit at by an opponent without getting disturbed. Even if an adversary lashes out thinking he'll score a blow, he won't be able to hit you as long as that margin is there.

A sword that fails to hit its target is a dead sword; you reach over it to strike the winning blow. Your adversary's initiative having missed its mark, you turn the tables around and get the first blow in on your adversary.

Once you've struck a blow, the thing is not to let your adversary even raise his hands. If you become occupied thinking about what to do after striking, the next blow will surely be struck by your opponent.

If you are inattentive here, you will lose. When your mind dallies on the blow you've just struck, you get hit by your opponent, making naught of your initiative. When you strike a blow, don't let your mind linger on whether or not it's effective; strike again and again, over and over, even four or five times. The thing is not to let your adversary even raise his head.

As for victory, it is determined by a single stroke of the sword.

> There is a double drawback to a blow that doesn't land, beyond the mere fact that it doesn't reach its target. One is that effort is required to recover poise after missing a blow, draining more energy than the delivery of the blow itself. The other is that missing a blow creates an opening in your defense, leaving you vulnerable to counterattack. That is why the missed blow is called the sword stroke of death, or the deadly stroke, because in a real fight one miss can be fatal. Thus a feint or a tentative attack is not only for the purpose of reading an adversary's defense, but also for inducing an adversary to launch a futile offensive and so set himself up for a fatal counterattack.

Three Rhythms

One rhythm is a simultaneous strike. Another is to close in and strike when the adversary's sword is raised. The third is to cross over and strike when the adversary's sword is lowered.

Matching rhythm is bad; incongruent rhythm is considered good. If your rhythm matches, that makes it easier for an opponent to use his sword. If your rhythm is in congruent, the adversary's sword is rendered useless.

You should strike in such a way as to make it difficult for opponents to use their swords. Whether closing in or crossing over, you should strike arhythmically. In general and in particular, a rhythm that can be tapped into is bad.

Tapping into a rhythm means aligning with it and thereby reading it, so as to be able to find an opening to strike. Another aspect of tapping into a rhythm is energetic, amplifying one's own force by riding with the rhythm of an opponent. Incongruity, or absence of rhythm, frustrates an adversary's strategy by foiling predictability, and drains the opponent's energy by interrupting continuity and deflecting momentum. This technique is further elaborated in the following section.

Small Rhythm to Large Rhythm, Large Rhythm to Small Rhythm

When an opponent uses his sword in a large rhythm, you should use yours with a small rhythm. If the opponent uses a small rhythm, you should use a large rhythm. Here too the idea is to use your sword in such a way that the rhythm is incongruent with that of your opponent. If he gets into your rhythm, it becomes easier for the adversary to use his sword.

For example, because an expert song goes over the intervals without lapsing into a fixed pattern, a mediocre drummer cannot drum to it. Just as it is hard to sing and drum if you put a mediocre drummer with an expert singer, or a mediocre singer with an expert drummer, to go at opponents in such a way as to make it hard for them to strike is called using a small rhythm to a large rhythm and a large rhythm to a small rhythm.

Even if a mediocre singer tries to handle a grandiose rhythm fluently, or an expert drummer tries to tap a little rhythm lightly, it will not be effective. And if an expert singer sings lightly, a mediocre drummer will fall behind and be unable to keep time.

An expert bird hunter shows the bird his pole, shaking it to make it jiggle, smoothly using that as a means to spear the prey. The bird, mesmerized by the rhythm of the jiggling pole, flaps its wings trying to take off but is unable to take off and thus gets speared.

You should act in a rhythm different from opponents. If your rhythm is incongruent, you can wade right in without your own defenses being crossed.

Such a state of mind should also be savored as an object of reflective study.

According to commentary, a "large rhythm" refers to attacking with a shout and a slash, while a "small rhythm" refers to acting swiftly with the movement of the eye focus. Again, the point of using a rhythm different from the adversary is to jam his offense while unraveling his defense, draining his energy while preserving your own. The following section emphasizes the importance of reading an adversary's rhythm.

Noting the Tempo

Whether in song or dance, without knowing the tempo neither can be performed. There must also be a sense of tempo in martial arts. Seeing with certainty how an adversary's sword is working, how he is handling it, to discern what is in his mind requires the same sense as mastery of the tempos of song and dance. When you know your opponent's moves and manners well, you can make your own maneuvers freely.

Sun-tzu's The Art of War *says, "If you know others and know yourself, you will not be imperiled in a hundred battles."*

Techniques I

1. Accompanying a blow of the sword.

2. Three inches between opposing sides.

3. Sneaking in quickly.

4. Focusing the eyes on the elbows in the upper position.

5. Circling sword; keeping an eye on both right and left.

6. Reckoning the three-foot margin.

The above six items are learned by working with a teacher and must be taught by word of mouth. They are not completely revealed in writing.

When you use such techniques to launch various preliminary strikes and to project appearances with covert intentions, and yet your adversary remains unruffled and refuses to make a move, remaining secure in a passive waiting mode, when you then sneak into the range of the sword, slipping right up to your adversary, and he can no longer hold back and shifts into the aggressive mode, then you induce the adversary to take the initiative, whereupon you let him hit out at you, and thus you strike him down.

In any case, you can't win unless your opponent lashes out. Even if an opponent lashes out at you, if you have properly learned how to gauge the margin of safety where you are out of reach, you will not get suddenly struck. Having practiced this step thoroughly, you can fearlessly slip right up to an adversary, get him to lash out, and then turn the tables on him to win. This is the sense of being a step ahead of the one who takes the initiative.

"Accompanying a blow of the sword" means striking as your opponent strikes.

"Three inches between opposing sides" means that a margin of three inches is enough to secure victory; three inches away from the tip of the opponent's sword on defense, three inches into the opponent's physical sphere on offense.

"Sneaking in quickly" means rapidly closing in on an opponent through an opening, getting within the arc of the sword to render it ineffective while maneuvering up close.

"Focusing the eyes on the elbows in the upper position" means watching the opponent's elbows when he's raised his sword over his head, because movement of the elbows will signal an imminent strike.

"Circling one's sword, rotating it at the hilt, while watching right and left," is a defensive maneuver to keep oneself covered while being able to shift fluidly into offense if a gap opens up in response to the circling sword.

"Reckoning the three-foot margin" means gauging the distance between oneself and one's opponent so as to be able to slip out of striking range and then immediately slip back in, as when one induces the opponent to lash out vainly then crosses over to strike the opening gap.

Techniques II

1. The major opus, including the initial assault; this must be communicated by word of mouth.
2. Sustained attention, used in both aggressive and passive modes; this must be communicated by word of mouth.
3. The one-cubit margin of a short sword.
4. The presence of both aggressive and passive modes when attacking: this should be understood as the body being in the aggressive mode with the sword in the passive mode.

The above items cannot be mastered unless learned by working with a teacher and communicated by word of mouth. It is impossible to express them well in writing.

The "major opus" means observing an opponent's tendencies, then using that to draw out an attack, opening up a gap in the adversary's defense so as to be able to strike successfully with a counterattack.

"Sustained attention" means keeping the eyes focused throughout a duel, not letting shifts in the action cause diversion or distraction.

The "one-cubit margin of the short sword" refers to a distance of a cubit from each shoulder; a samurai typically carried a long sword and a short sword. When an adversary on the attack enters within the one-cubit margin, his neck can be reached with a short sword.

The use of "both aggressive and passive modes," the body aggressive with the sword passive, refers to the active use of body language to elicit an adversary's moves, while keeping one's sword in a position of ready reserve to be able to follow up on an opening at once.

Hearing the Sound of Wind and Water

This science, in any case, is all about how to win by getting your adversary to take the initiative, launching various preliminary blows and shifting strategically, based on tactical ploys.

Before facing off you should assume your opponent to be in the aggressive mode and should not fail to be attentive. Mental preparation is essential. If you do not assume your adversary to be in the aggressive mode, the techniques you have been learning hitherto will be of no avail when you are assailed with great vehemence the instant the duel starts.

Once you face off, it is essential to put your mind, body, and feet in the aggressive mode while putting your hands in the waiting mode. Be sure to pay attention to what is there. This is what is meant by the saying, "Take what is there in hand." If you do not observe with utmost calm, the sword techniques you have learned will not be useful.

As for the matter of "hearing the sound of wind and water," this means being calm and quiet on the surface while keeping energy aggressive underneath. Wind has no sound;

it produces sound when it strikes objects. Thus wind is silent when it blows up above. When it makes contact with objects like trees and bamboo below, the sound it produces is noisy and frantic.

Water also has no sound when it is falling from above; it makes a frantic sound below when it comes down and hits things.

Using these images as illustrations, the point is to be calm and quiet on the surface, while keeping energy aggressive underneath. These are images of outwardly being extremely serene, unruffled, and calm, while inwardly being aggressively watchful.

It is bad for body, hands, and feet to be hurried. The aggressive and passive modes should be paired, one inward and one outward; it is bad to settle into just one mode. It is imperative to reflect on the sense of yin and yang alternating.

Movement is yang, stillness is yin. Yin and yang interchange, inside and outside. When yang moves inwardly, you're outwardly still, in the yin mode; when you are inwardly yin, movement appears outwardly.

In this way, in martial arts as well, you activate your energy inwardly, constantly attentive, while remaining outwardly calm and unruffled. This is yang moving within while yin is quiet without. This is in accord with the pattern of Nature.

Furthermore, when outwardly intensely aggressive, if you are internally calm, so your inner mind is not captured by the outside, then you will not be outwardly wild. If you move both inwardly and outwardly at once, you become wild. The aggressive and passive modes, movement and stillness, should be made to alternate inside and outside.

Keeping the inner mind attentive, like a duck swimming on the water, calm above while paddling below, when this practice builds up, the inner mind and the outside merge together so that inside and outside become one, with no barrier at all. To arrive at this state is the supreme attainment.

> The Art of War *by Sun-tzu says, "A good attack is one against which an enemy does not know where to defend, while a good defense is one against which an enemy does not know where to attack.... Thus a militia has no permanently fixed configuration, no constant form. Those who are able to seize victory by adapting to opponents are called experts."*

Sickness

To be obsessed even with winning is sickness. To be obsessed even with using martial arts is sickness. To be obsessed with showing all one has learned is sickness too.

To be obsessed with offense is sickness; to be obsessed with defense is also sickness.

To become rigidly obsessed with getting rid of sickness is also sickness.

To fix the mind obsessively on anything is considered sickness. Since all of these various sicknesses are in the mind, the thing is to tune the mind by getting rid of such afflictions.

Eliminating Sickness: Elementary and Advanced Levels
Elementary Level

"Free from thought having gotten into thought, free from fixation having gotten fixated." The meaning of this is that the intention to get rid of thought is a thought. To intend to eliminate sickness in the mind is getting into thought.

Now then, the expression "sickness" also means obsessive thought. To think of getting rid of sickness is also thought. Thus you use thought to get rid of thought. When rid of thoughts, you're free from thought, so this is called being free from thought having gotten into thought.

When you take thought to get rid of the sickness that remains in thought, after that the thought of removal and the thoughts to be removed both disappear. This is what is known as using a wedge to extract a wedge.

When you can't get a wedge out, if you drive in another wedge to ease the pressure, then the first wedge comes out. Once the stuck wedge comes out, the wedge driven in after isn't left there. When sickness is gone, the thought of getting rid of sickness is no longer there, so this is called being free from thought having gotten into thought.

To think of getting rid of sickness is fixation on sickness, but if you use that fixation to get rid of sickness, the fixation will not remain. So this is called being free from fixation having gotten fixated.

Advanced Level

At the advanced level, to have no thought of getting rid of sickness at all is getting rid of sickness. To think of riddance is itself sickness. Letting sickness be while living in the midst of sickness is to be rid of sickness.

Thinking of eliminating sickness occurs because sickness is still in the mind. Therefore sickness doesn't depart, and whatever you do and think is done with fixation, so there can be no higher value in it.

How is this to be understood? The two levels, elementary and advanced, have been set up for this purpose. You cultivate the state of mind of the elementary level, and when this cultivation builds up, fixation departs on its own, without your intending to eliminate it.

Sickness means fixation. In Buddhism, fixation is rejected. Mendicants who are free of fixation are unaffected even if they mix with ordinary society; whatever they do is done freely and independently, stopping where it naturally should.

Masters of the arts cannot be called adepts as long as they have not left behind fixation on their various skills. Dust and dirt adhere to an unpolished gem, but a perfectly polished gem will not be stained even if it falls into mud. Polishing the gem of your mind by spiritual cultivation so that it is impervious to stain, having left sickness alone and given up concern, you can act as you will.

> *The Zen concept of fixation as sickness is elucidated with exceptional clarity by the famous Chinese Chan master Foyan, who lived from 1060 to 1120:*
>
> *"In the* Heroic Progress Scripture, *Buddha described fifty kinds of meditation sickness. Now I'm telling you that you need to be free from sickness to attain realization.*
>
> *"According to my school, there are only two kinds of sickness. One is to mount a donkey to go looking for a donkey. The other one is to be unwilling to dismount after having mounted the donkey.*
>
> *"You say it is certainly a serious sickness to ride a donkey in search of a donkey. I say you needn't find a spiritually sharp individual to recognize this right away and eliminate the sickness of seeking so the mad mind stops.*

"The sickness that is most difficult to treat is to be unwilling to dismount the donkey after you have found it and gotten on it. I tell you that you need not mount the donkey—you are the donkey! The whole world is the donkey—how can you mount it? If you mount it, you can be sure the sickness won't leave; if you don't mount it, the whole universe is wide open.

"When the two sicknesses are gone, and there is nothing on your mind, then you are called a wayfarer."

The Normal Mind

A monk asked an ancient worthy, "What is the Way?"

The ancient worthy replied, "The normal mind is the Way."

This story contains a principle that applies to all the arts. Asked what the Way is, the ancient worthy replied that the normal mind is the Way. This is indeed supreme. This is the state where the sicknesses of the mind are all gone and one has become normal in mind, free from sickness even in the midst of sickness.

To apply this to worldly matters, suppose you are shooting with a bow and you think you are shooting while you are shooting; then the aim of your bow will be inconsistent and unsteady. If you are conscious of wielding your sword when wielding your sword, your offense will be unstable. If you are conscious of writing while writing, your pen will be unsteady. Even when you play the harp, the tune will be off if you're conscious of playing.

When an archer forgets consciousness of shooting and shoots in a normal frame of mind, as if unoccupied, the bow will be steady. When using a sword or riding a horse too, you do not "wield a sword" or "ride a horse." And you do not "write"; you do not "play music." When you do everything in the normal state of mind as it is when totally unoccupied, then everything goes smoothly and easily.

Whatever you do as your Way, if you keep it in your heart as the only thing of importance, then it is not the Way. When you have nothing in your heart, then you are on the Way. Whatever you do, if you do it with nothing in your heart, it works out easily.

This is like the way everything is reflected in a mirror clearly precisely because of the constant formless clarity of the mirror's reflectivity. The heart of those on the Way is like a mirror, empty and clear, mindless yet not failing to accomplish anything. This is the normal mind. One who does everything with this normal mind is called an adept.

Whatever you do, if you keep the idea of doing it before you, and do it with single-minded concentration, then you will be inconsistent. You'll do it well once, but then when you think that is fine, you'll do it badly. Or you may do it well twice and then do it badly again. If you are glad you did it well twice and badly but once, you will then do it badly again, with no consistency at all. This is because of acting with the thought of doing it well.

When the effects of exercise build up unawares and practice accumulates, thoughts of wishing to develop skill quickly disappear quietly, and you naturally become free from conscious thoughts whatever you do, like a wooden puppet performing.

At this point you don't even know yourself. When your body, feet, and hands act without your doing anything in your mind, you don't miss ten times out of ten.

Even then, you will miss if it gets on your mind at all. When you are not consciously mindful, you will score every time. Not being consciously mindful does not, however, mean total mindlessness. It just means a normal mind.

The Chinese Chan master Foyan cited above also quotes the same story about the normal mind to illustrate freedom from the sickness of fixation: "When Zhaozhou asked Nanquan, 'What is the Way?' Nanquan replied, 'The normal mind is the Way.' All at once Zhaozhou stopped his hasty search, recognized the sickness of 'Zen Masters' and the sickness of 'Buddhas,' and passed through it all. After that he traveled all over and had no peer anywhere because of his recognition of sicknesses."

The earlier Taoist classic Liezi, *composed in the third to fourth centuries CE and containing a considerable mixture of Buddhist thought, features numerous precursors to Zen methodology, including the imagery of archery as used by Yagyu to illustrate the Way of naturalness:*

"Rebel Resister Lie performed some archery for Elder Stupid Nobody. Drawing the bow fully with a cup of water on his arm, he shot one arrow after another in continuous succession, still as a statue all the while.

"Elder Stupid Nobody said, 'This is deliberate shooting, not spontaneous shooting. Suppose we climbed a high mountain and stood on a precipice overlooking an abyss — could you shoot then?'

"So they climbed a high mountain, where Nobody went out on a precipice. Standing with his back to the abyss,

heels hanging off the ledge, he beckoned to Rebel Resister to join him. Rebel Resister fell prostrate on the ground, running with sweat.

"Elder Stupid Nobody said, 'Complete people gaze into the blue sky above, plunge into the center of the earth below, and run freely in the eight directions without even a change of mood. Now you have a fearful expression of aversion—your inner state must be very uneasy!'"

Like a Wooden Man Facing Flowers and Birds

This is a saying of Layman Pang: "Like a wooden man facing flowers and birds." Though his eyes are on the flowers and birds, his mind does not stir at the flowers and birds. Because a wooden man has no mind, it is not moved; this is perfectly logical. But how can a person with a mind become like a wooden man?

The wooden man is a metaphor. As a human being with a mind, one cannot be exactly like a wooden manikin. As a human being, one cannot be like bamboo or wood. Even though you do see flowers, you do not see them by reproducing the consciousness of seeing the flowers.

The point of the saying is simply to see innocently, with the normal mind. When you shoot, you don't shoot by reproducing the consciousness of shooting. In other words, you shoot with the normal mind.

The normal mind is called unminding. If you change the normal mind and instead reproduce another consciousness, your form will also change, so you will stir both internally and externally. If you do everything with a stirring mind, nothing will be as it should.

Even in a mere matter of speaking a word, people will praise it if and only if your manner of saying it is unstirring and unshakable. What they call the unstirring mind of the Buddhas seems truly sublime.

> *Layman Pang was a lay Chan master. His enlightenment verse, illustrating the Chan notion of normalcy, is very famous in sectarian annals:*
>
> *"My everyday affairs are no different,*
>
> *Only I myself harmonize.*
>
> *Nowhere is grasped or rejected,*
>
> *Nowhere for or against.*
>
> *Who thinks crimson and purple noble?*
>
> *The green mountains haven't a speck of dust.*
>
> *Spiritual powers, wondrous actions—*
>
> *Hauling water, carrying wood."*
>
> *Layman Pang's main teacher, Mazu, was one of the most illustrious Chan masters of all time. He explained the normal mind, an expression he himself may have coined, in these terms: "If you want to understand the Way directly, the normal mind is the Way. What I mean by the normal mind is the mind without artificiality, without subjective judgments, without grasping or rejection."*

The Free Mind

Master Zhongfeng said, "Embody the free-minded mind." There are elementary and advanced levels of applying this saying.

When you let the mind go, it stops where it has gone. Therefore the first level of practice is to get it to come back each time, so that the mind does not stay anywhere. When you strike a blow of the sword and your mind lingers where you struck, this teaching has you get it to return to you.

At the advanced level, the message is to let your mind be free to go wherever it will. Having made it so it will not stop and linger anywhere even when set free, you release your mind.

To embody the free-minded mind means that you are not free or independent as long as you use the mind that releases the mind to rope the mind and keep dragging it back. The mind that does not stop and linger anywhere even when set free is called the free-minded mind.

When you embody this free-minded mind, then independence is possible in actual practice. You are not independent as long as you are holding on to a halter. Even dogs and cats should be raised unleashed. Cats and dogs cannot be raised properly if they are tied up all the time.

People who read Confucian books dwell on the word *seriousness* as if it were the ultimate, spending their whole lives on seriousness, thus making their minds like leashed cats.

There is seriousness in Buddhism too; scripture speaks of being single-minded and undistracted, which corresponds to seriousness. It means setting the mind on one thing and not letting it scatter elsewhere.

There are, of course, passages that say, "We seriously declare of the Buddha . . . ," and we speak of single-mindedly and seriously paying respects when we face an icon of a Buddha in what we call reverent obeisance.

These are consistent with the meaning of seriousness. They are, however, in any case, expedient means for controlling mental distraction. A well-governed mind does not need expedients to control it.

When we chant, "Great Sage, Immovable One," with our posture correct and our palms joined, in our minds we visualize the image of the Immovable One. At this time, our three modes of action—physical, verbal, and mental—are balanced, and we are single-minded and undistracted. This is called the equality of the three mysteries. In other words, this has the same import as seriousness.

Seriousness corresponds to a quality of the basic mind, yet it is a state of mind that lasts only so long as it is practiced. When we relax our reverential gesture and stop chanting buddha-names, the image of Buddha in our minds also disappears. What then remains is the former distracted mind. This is not a thoroughly pacified mind.

People who have successfully managed to pacify their minds once do not purify their thoughts, words, and deeds— they are unstained even as they mingle with the dust of the world. Even if they are active all day, they are unmoved, just as the moon reflected in the water does not move even though millions of waves roll one after another.

This is the realm of people who have attained Buddhism completely; I have recorded it here under the instruction of a teacher of that doctrine.

Zhongfeng Mingben (1263–1323) was one of a comparatively small number of distinguished Chan teachers of the Yuan dynasty, when esoteric Buddhism was imported into China from Central Asia by Mongol overlords and many of the native Chan schools converted to Taoism. Zhongfeng is particularly noted for the use of Chan sayings for concentration, but he emphasized that this is just an expedient and the real goal is normalcy in the Chan sense: "Chan is the teaching of the true ground of mind. If you are sure you want to comprehend the great matter of life and death, you should know that with a single thought of doubt or confusion you fall into the realm of demons."

The distinction Yagyu draws between teaching and training, and his emphasis on naturalness rather than coercion in real education represent a level of sophistication that, while characteristic of Buddhist psychology, was never implemented on a wide scale in Japan. Although there is a great deal of literature on this subject in modern times, moreover, mechanical training and coercion remain the mainstays of official educational systems even in the most liberal societies today.

The use of the terms "seriousness" or "respectfulness" to mean single-mindedness is characteristic of neo-Confucianism, which developed in China under the influence of Chan Buddhism. In Yagyu's time, neo-Confucianism was established as the standard curriculum in secular education, and many Zen monks left religious orders to become lay Confucian scholars. Yagyu's critique of Confucianism is classically Buddhist in its focus on practical method.

The interpretation of ritual behavior in terms of intended psychological effect is also a Zen tradition, though this level of understanding is unknown to indoctrinated followers. The expression "equality of the three mysteries" derives from esoteric Shingon Buddhism, which emphasizes the attainment of buddhahood in this very body. The three mysteries are thought, word, and deed, and their equality is with those of the cosmic Buddha Vairocana, the Illuminator, or Great Sun Buddha. In formal Shingon Buddhism, this identity is expressed through symbolic rites, as illustrated here. In Zen Buddhism, this identity is realized through awakening to the universal ground of mind.

This essentialist Zen approach is what Yagyu alludes to in his final statement here. His note that it was made under the direction of a teacher is a disclaimer of personal Zen mastery.

Book 2

The Life-Giving Sword

~

Even If There Are a Hundred Positions, You Win with Just One

The point of this is perceiving abilities and intentions. Even if a hundred or a thousand manners of swordplay are taught and learned, including all sorts of positions of the body and the sword, the perception of abilities and intentions alone is to be considered discernment. Even if your opponent has a hundred postures and you have a hundred stances, the ultimate point is solely in the perception of abilities and intentions.

This is passed on secretly, so it is not written in the proper characters, but with code words having the same sound.

Every possible move may have its countermove, but the ability to match a move at the right moment depends on direct perception and instant response, while the ability to outguess and outmaneuver an adversary depends on intuiting intention. This same basic principle also applies to civil affairs, wherein perception of abilities and intentions is crucial to effective organization and management.

Both the concept of perception as paramount and the practice of clearing the mind to achieve accurate perception are found in the ancient Chinese strategic classic The Master of Demon Valley:

"You need to be even-minded and calm yourself in order to listen to people's statements, examine their affairs, assess myriad things, and distinguish relative merits. Even if you repudiate specific matters, see their subtleties and know their types. If you are searching into people and live in their midst, you can measure their abilities and see into their intentions, with never a failure to tally. Therefore knowledge begins from knowing yourself; after that you can know others."

The Rhythm of Existence and Nonexistence plus
The Existence of Both the Existent and the Nonexistent

These expressions refer to the custom of using the terms existence and nonexistence in reference to abilities and intentions. When evident, they are existent; when concealed, they are nonexistent. This existence and nonexistence, hidden and manifest, refer to perceptions of abilities and intentions. They are in the hand that grips the sword.

There are analyses of existence and nonexistence in Buddhism; here we use them analogously. Ordinary people see the existent but not the nonexistent. In perception of abilities and intentions we see both the existent and the nonexistent.

The fact is that existence and nonexistence are both there. When there is existence, you strike the existent; when there is nonexistence, you strike the nonexistent. Moreover, you strike the nonexistent without waiting for its existence, and strike the existent without waiting for its nonexistence; hence it is said that the existent and nonexistent both exist.

In a commentary on the classic of Lao-tzu, there is something called "always existent, always nonexistent." Existence is always there, and nonexistence is always there as well. When concealed, the existent becomes nonexistent; when revealed, the nonexistent becomes existent.

To illustrate, when a duck is floating on top of water, it is "present," while when it dives under water, it is "absent." Thus even when we think something exists, once it is concealed, it is nonexistent. And even if we think something is nonexistent, when it is revealed, it exists. Therefore existence and nonexistence just mean concealment and manifestation; the substance is the same. Thus existence and nonexistence are always there.

In Buddhism, they speak of fundamental nonexistence and fundamental existence. When people die, the existent is concealed; when people are born, the nonexistent is manifested. The substance is eternal.

There are existence and nonexistence in the hand that grips the sword. This is a trade secret. This is called perception of ability and intention. When you have hidden your hand, what you have there is concealed. When you turn your palm face up, what was not there is revealed.

Even so, without personal instruction these words are hard to understand.

When there is existence, you should see the existent and strike it. When there is nonexistence, you should see the nonexistent and strike it. That is why we say that the existent and nonexistent both exist.

If you misperceive the existence and nonexistence of abilities and intentions, you will not attain victory even if you use a hundred techniques to the fullest. Every sort of martial art is consummated in this one step.

Existence, or presence, indicates externalization or actualization of ability and intent. Nonexistence, or absence, indicates concealment or latency of ability and intent. To see existence and strike it means to parry a move and counter; to see nonexistence and strike it means to foil a move before it is made. If attention to immediate action obscures alertness to potential plotting, it will be impossible to outmaneuver an adversary. On the other hand, if fixation on foresight and preemption distracts attention from the present, this creates gaps in defense.

Therefore this dynamic balance of awareness, at once attentive to the evident and the unseen, is crucial to all martial arts. It is taught secretly in the sense that verbal description alone does not convey the personal experience necessary for actual understanding and true realization. This principle of martial arts is analogous to the Zen dictum, "The secret is in yourself." That is to say, the potentiality to which the teaching refers has to be experienced personally to be comprehended. This is so by nature, not by artificial esoterism.

The Moon in the Water and Its Reflection

There is a certain distance between an opponent and yourself at which you will not get hit by the opponent's sword. Martial arts are employed from outside this space.

To get close to an opponent by striding into this space, or slipping into it, is called *the moon in the water*, likened to the moon sending its reflection into a body of water.

One should engage an opponent only after having figured out the standpoint of the *moon in the water* before facing off. The measurement of the spacing has to be passed on by word of mouth.

> *The principle of assessing a margin of safety is also essential to large-scale warfare.* The Art of War *says, "The ancients who were skilled in combat first became invincible, and in that condition awaited vulnerability on the part of enemies. . . . Those skilled at defense hide in the deepest depths of the earth; those skilled at offense maneuver in the highest heights of the sky. . . . Those who are skilled in combat take a stand on an invincible ground without losing sight of opponents' vulnerabilities."*

The Inscrutable Sword

The inscrutable sword is a matter of utmost importance. There is a way to wear it oneself as an inscrutable sword. When one carries it with oneself, the character for sword in *inscrutable sword* is written and understood as *sword*. Whether positioned to the right or the left, as long as the sword has not left the inscrutable state there is meaning in the use of the character for *sword*.

In reference to adversaries, the character *ken* for sword should be written and understood as the word *ken* for see. Since you are to see the position of inscrutable swords clearly in order to wade in slashing, the seeing is essential. Thus there is meaning in the character *ken* for *seeing.*

> *The inscrutable sword is the sword in a passive or "quiet" state of reserve. This implies both position and potential, as well as covert intention. In code language, it is written and understood as "sword" in reference to one's own reserve capacity and strategy, while written and understood as "seeing" in reference to the tactical need to perceive opponents' reserve capacity and strategy in order to see an opportune moment to launch an assault.*

Explanation of the Characters
Spirit and *Wonder*—Meaning Inscrutable

The spirit is within, the wonder appears outwardly. This is called a divine wonder, or an inscrutable marvel.

For example, because there is the spirit of tree in a tree, its flowers blossom fragrantly, its foliage turns green, its branches and leaves flourish—this is called the wonder.

If you break wood down, you don't see anything you may call the spirit of tree, yet if there were no spirit, the flowers and foliage would not emerge.

This is also true of the human spirit; though you cannot open up the body to see something you may call the spirit, it is by virtue of the existence of the spirit within that you perform all sorts of actions.

When you settle your spirit where your sword is inscrutable, all sorts of marvels appear in your hands and feet, causing flowers to blossom in battle.

The spirit is the master of the mind. The spirit resides within, employing the mind outside.

This mind, moreover, employs energy. Employing energy in external activities on behalf of the spirit, if this mind lingers in one place, its function is deficient. So it is essential to make sure that the mind is not fixated on one point.

For example, when the master of a house, staying at home, sends an employee out on an errand, if the employee stays where he goes and does not return, he will be missing for further duties. In the same way, if your mind lingers on things and does not return to its original state, then your ability in martial arts will slip.

For this reason, the matter of not fixating the mind on one point applies to everything, not only martial arts.

There are two understandings, spirit and mind.

As in certain other places in his handbook, the vocabulary and imagery Yagyu uses here is more akin to Chinese Taoist and martial arts traditions than Zen spirituality. The classic Master of Demon Valley *says,*

"If the mind lacks appropriate technique, there will inevitably be failure to penetrate. With this penetration, five energies are nurtured. The task is a matter of sheltering the spirit. This is called development. Development involves five energies, including will, thought, spirit, and character. Spirit is the unifying leader. Calmness and harmony nurture energy. When energy attains the right harmony, then will, thought, spirit, and character do not deteriorate, and these four facets of force and power all thereby survive and remain. This is called spiritual development ending up in the body. . . .

"Development of will is for when the energy of mind does not reach its intended object. When you have some desire, your will dwells on it and intends it. Will is a functionary of desire; when you have many desires, your mind is scattered. When your mind is scattered, your will deteriorates. When your will deteriorates, then thought does not attain its object."

Eliminating Sickness
Three Things: Sickness in Opponents

Yagyu does not elaborate on these items in his book, but commentary defines the three things as intending to strike, intending to prevail, and intending to parry. These three are points at which attention is apt to fail and sickness—fixation—is apt to emerge. This happens, commentary explains, when one's composure is disrupted by one's own movements. From the point of view of offense, the aim of identifying these three things is to perceive the emergence of attention failure and fixation in opponents, thus seizing the opportunity to strike.

First Glance
Maintenance of Rhythm

These are to be transmitted by word of mouth.

The "first glance" refers to immediate assessment of the situation at first glance; "keeping rhythm" refers to unrelenting follow-through. These have to be transmitted verbally because the directions have to be given by an expert in the process of actual practice, where theoretical explanation is too indirect.

Stride

Your stride should not be too quick or too slow. Steps should be taken in an unruffled, casual manner.

It is bad to go too far or not far enough; take the mean. When you go too quickly, it's because of being scared or flustered; when you go too slowly, it's because of being timid and frightened.

The desired state is one in which you are not upset at all. Usually people will blink when something brushes by their open eyes, even a fan; this is normal, and blinking does not indicate being upset. If you didn't blink at all even if someone swung at you repeatedly to startle you, that would actually mean you were upset. Consciously determining to hold back natural blinking indicates a far more disturbed mind than blinking does.

The undisturbed mind is normal. If something comes at your eyes, you unconsciously blink. This is the state of not being upset. What is essential is the psychological state in which you don't lose the normal mind. To try not to stir is to have stirred; movement is an unalterable principle. For a waterwheel, it is normal to turn; if it doesn't turn, that's abnormal. For people to blink is normal; not blinking indicates mental disturbance.

It is good to take steps in a normal manner, without altering your normal frame of mind. This is the state where neither your appearance nor your mind is upset.

Intentional effort to suppress agitation expends energy, generates stiffness and tension, and projects fear. A Zen classic says, "If you try to stop movement, the stopping produces more movement." This combination of nega-

tive factors weakens and retards response, thereby increasing vulnerability to attack. The purpose of naturalness is to remain relaxed yet in control, in command of one's faculties, flexible and alert, not frozen, able to shift from passive to aggressive mode in an instant, all the while projecting an air of aloofness and insouciance to discourage and intimidate the opponent.

The Unifying Principle
The Mental Attitude in a Face-Off Is as When Facing a Spear
What to Do When You Have No Sword

The Unifying Principle is a code word in martial arts. In the context of the art of war in general, it means being free in every possible way.

The critical thing is what happens when you are hard pressed. The principle of one means you keep that clearly in mind, pay close attention, and make sure you do not get caught unprepared in a pinch.

The attention employed in face-to-face confrontation with swords when an opponent's stab nearly reaches you, or when a spear is thrust into the cubit margin of safety, is called the unifying principle.

This is the attention employed at times such as when you are being attacked with your back to a wall and can't extricate yourself. It should be understood as a most critical and most difficult situation.

When you have no sword, the one-cubit margin of safety is quite impossible to maintain if you fix your eyes on one spot, let your mind linger on one place, and fail to keep up sustained watchfulness.

Keeping things like this in mind is a secret, referred to as the unifying principle.

Buddhist metaphysics represents all phenomena as based on one principle. This principle is variously called interdependent origination or emptiness, and realization of this underlying principle is considered essential to Zen. In the context of martial arts, the principle of interdependent origination means that every element of an interchange — the weaponry, the terrain, the particulars of posture and movement, the state of mind of the participants — are all in a state of dynamic interplay, each affecting and affected by every other element involved. Alertness to the flux of this total dynamic is called the unifying principle because it encompasses all aspects of the event at once.

In metaphysics, the principle of interdependent origin is identified with emptiness in the sense that whatever is dependent on something else has no intrinsic substance or nature of its own. That is called emptiness in an objective sense; its subjective realization is not only intellectual understanding, but in the experience of open awareness that is not fixated on any object. It is this open awareness, enabling the mind to take in the whole scene of the immediate moment without attention being caught anywhere, that is valued in the context of martial arts as the unifying principle.

The One-Foot Margin on Both Sides

When both swords are the same size, attention is to be concentrated as with no sword.

The weapons on both sides are one foot away from the body. With a margin of one foot, you can slip and parry. It is dangerous to get closer than this distance.

This Is the Ultimate
The First Sword

This is the ultimate is a manner of referring to what is supremely consummate. *The first sword* does not refer literally to a sword; *the first sword* is a code expression for seeing incipient movement on the part of an opponent. The expression *the critical first sword* means that seeing what an opponent is trying to do is the first sword in the ultimate sense.

Perception of an opponent's impulse and incipient action being understood as the first sword, the blow that strikes according to his action is to be understood as the second sword.

Making this the basis, you use it in various ways. Perceiving abilities and intentions, the moon in the water, the inscrutable sword, and sicknesses make four; with the working of hands and feet, altogether they make five. These are learned as *five observations, one seeing.*

To perceive abilities and intentions is called *one seeing.* The other four are called observations because they are held in mind. Perceiving with the eyes is called seeing, perceiving with the mind is called observation. This means contemplation in the mind.

The reason we do not call this four observations and one seeing, speaking instead of five observations, is that we use five observations as an inclusive term, of which one — perceiving abilities and intentions — is called *one seeing.*

Perceiving abilities and intentions; the moon in the water; the inscrutable sword; sickness; body, hands, and feet — these are five items. Four of these are observed mentally, while the perception of abilities and intentions is seen with the eyes and is called *one seeing.*

This emphasis on the importance of perception as the basis of effective action is applied to all endeavors, civil as well as military, in the ancient Chinese strategic classic Master of Demon Valley:

"Focusing the mind's eye is for determining impending perils. Events have natural courses, people have successes and failures; it is imperative to examine movements signaling impending perils. . . . The mind's eye is knowledge, focus is practical action. . . . When you can stop opponents from adapting and unsettle their order, this is called great success. . . . Use tactics that divide power and disperse momentum in order to see the mind's eye of others. Threaten their vulnerabilities and you can be sure about them. . . . Skillful focus of the mind's eye is like splitting open a ten-thousand-foot dam and letting the water gush out."

Analysis of the Moon in the Water
The Inscrutable Sword
Sickness
Body, Hands, and Feet

The moon in the water is a matter of the choice of the physical setting of a duel.

The inscrutable sword is a matter of the choice of your own location.

"Body, hands, and feet" refers to watching what opponents do, and to your own movements.

Therefore, the ultimate point is solely to see whether or not there is ability and intention. The other four are general.

Getting rid of sickness is for the purpose of seeing abilities and intentions. As long as you aren't rid of sickness, you'll be distracted by it and fail to see. When you fail to see, you lose.

Sickness means sickness of mind. Sickness of mind is when the mind tarries here and there. You should make sure not to let your mind linger where you have struck with your sword. This is a matter of letting go of the mind without abandoning it.

> As explained in the first section, "The Killing Sword," the "moon in the water" refers to slipping into killing range from outside the margin of safety. This depends not only on skill in perception and movement, but also on the features of the physical setting.
>
> The "inscrutable sword" is the sword in the passive state of reserve or quiescence, where there is no indication of intent or impulse. Expedient disposition of the sword in reserve depends in part on the lay of the land and the relative position of adversaries on the field of combat. The critical question is where reserve power can be stored in a given situation so as to be inscrutable to the enemy yet available for instant deployment.
>
> The sword master refers to fixation of attention by the Zen term of "sickness" because in the context of martial arts fixation is not simply a philosophical or psychological problem but a fatal breakdown. "Getting rid of sickness" means clearing the mind of fixations, thereby freeing attention to function more fully and fluidly in the present.
>
> "Letting go of the mind without abandoning it" means freeing the mind of fixations without losing concentration, attention, or control. This is typical Zen teaching.

If an adversary is positioned so that the tip of his sword is facing you, strike as he raises it. When you intend to strike an opponent, let him hit at you. As long as your adversary lashes out at you, you have as good as struck him.

> *When the adversary raises his sword, intending to go on the offense, this opens up a gap in his defense. Letting an opponent hit at you opens up gaps in defense that can be struck with a counterattack.*

Take up a moon-in-the-water position. After that, concentrate on your state of mind.

When you try to take up a position, if your adversary has already taken up a position, make that yours.

As long as the spacing doesn't change, the distance between you and your opponent remains the same even if your opponent approaches five feet or you approach five feet.

If others have taken up positions, it is best to let them take those positions for the time being. It is bad to get too wrapped up in jockeying for position. Keep your body buoyant.

> *A moon-in-the-water position is outside the opponent's range but close enough to slip in past his defenses. The margin of safety permits room for mental adjustment and physical maneuvering; when an adversary has already occupied a position, one makes it one's own mentally and physically by adopting a moon-in-the-water position according to context, so as to be able to maintain a distance that is safe but can be crossed instantly when a gap opens up. The energy saved by letting others have their positions can be reserved for this crossing; keeping the body buoyant implies the nimbleness to seize the moment to close in and strike.*

Footwork and disposition of the body should be such as not to slip out of the location of the inscrutable sword. This determination should be remembered all along, from even before facing off.

> *From the point of view of defensive maneuvers, it is critical to discern the adversary's reserve. From the point of view of both defense and offense, it is essential to know how to keep one's own reserve undetected yet always ready. If your reserve is undetected, your opponent can't tell where to strike or where to defend, not knowing whether or where there might be a gap in your defense and not being able to discern where or when you might launch an offense.*

Seeing the Inscrutable Sword: Distinctions of Three Levels

Seeing with the mind is considered basic. It is due to seeing from the mind that the eyes are also effective; therefore seeing with the eyes is subordinate to seeing with the mind.

Next after that is to see with your body, feet, and hands. Seeing with your body, feet, and hands means that you don't let your body, feet, or hands miss the inscrutable sword of an adversary.

Seeing with the mind is for the purpose of seeing with the eyes. Seeing with the eyes means aiming your feet and hands at the location of an adversary's inscrutable sword.

> *Seeing with the mind comes about through concentration; it refers to sensing movement in the opponent's mind before it is translated into physical movement. "Seeing with the body, feet, and hands" refers to sensing*

the energetic field of an adversary and responding adaptively to alterations in its configuration. In this way the sensitivities of the mind, senses, and physical body are coordinated to identify and inhibit the opponent's reserve and thus forestall an attack.

The Mind Is Like the Moon in the Water, the Body Is Like an Image in a Mirror

The sense in which these expressions are applied to martial arts is as follows.

Water reflects an image of the moon, a mirror reflects an image of a person's body. The reflection of things in the human mind is like the reflection of the moon in the water, reflecting instantaneously.

The location of the inscrutable sword is likened to water, your mind is likened to the moon. The mind should be reflected in the location of the inscrutable sword. When the mind shifts there, the body shifts to the location of the inscrutable sword. Where the mind goes, the body goes; the body follows the mind.

A mirror is also likened to the location of the inscrutable sword, in which case these expressions are used to mean moving your body to the location of the inscrutable sword like a reflection. The principle is not letting your hands and feet slip from the location of the inscrutable sword.

The reflection of the moon in the water is an instantaneous phenomenon. Even though it is way out in space, the moon casts its reflection in water the instant clouds disappear. The reflection doesn't descend from the sky in a gradual way, but is cast at once, before you can blink an eye. This is a simile for the way things reflect in people's minds as immediately as the moon reflects in a body of water.

Passages in Buddhist scripture saying the mind is as instantaneous as the moon reflected in water, or an image cast in a mirror, don't mean that the moon reflected in water appears to be there but actually is not; this simply refers to casting a reflection instantly from far away in the sky. A form being reflected in a mirror that immediately reflects whatever is before it, is also a simile for immediacy.

This is the way the human mind reflects in things. The mind may travel even as far as China in the blink of an eye. Just as you think you are dozing off, your dreams travel to your native village far away. The Buddha explained this kind of reflection of the mind as being like the moon in water or images in a mirror.

These expressions also apply to the same phenomenon in the context of martial arts. You should transfer your mind to the appropriate place like the moon reflecting in a body of water. Where the mind goes, the body goes; so once a face-off begins, you should shift your body to the appropriate spot like an image reflecting in a mirror. If you don't send your mind there beforehand in preparation, your body will not go.

In reference to place it is called *the moon in the water,* while in terms of the person it is *the inscrutable sword.* In either case, the sense of shifting the body, feet, and hands is the same.

A hasty attack is an exceptionally bad thing. You should press aggressively only after having properly prepared yourself mentally and having observed the situation thoroughly once the face-off has begun. It is essential not to get flustered.

The Zen exercise of clearing the mind enables one to stay alert to the instant, so that direct perception and immediate response are possible. When this is practiced with body awareness as well, it is possible to culti-

vate energetic sensing, which underlies the capacity to close a gap at once. On the defense, closing a gap means blocking an opening of one's own; on the offense, closing a gap means striking an opening in the adversary's defense. In either case it is essential to sense the config-urations and changes in the energy fields of both parties, where they are emptying and where they are filling. Mental clarity and physical buoyancy operate together to produce the sensitivity and responsiveness required to execute this strategy.

There are certain Zen koans that help to illustrate and induce the experiential basis of this capacity. One of them is found in the Congronglu *(Japanese* Shoyoroku*), or* Book of Serenity, *case 52: A Zen master asked a senior disciple, quoting from scripture, "'The true reality body of buddhas is like space, manifesting form in response to beings, like the moon in the water'—how do you explain the principle of response?" The disciple replied, "Like an ass looking into a well." The master said, "You've said a lot indeed, but you only said eighty percent." The disciple asked the teacher the same ques-tion; the teacher replied, "Like the well looking at the ass." This illustrates the difference between deliberate and spontaneous "moon in the water" maneuvering.*

The other koan is found in the Biyanlu *(Japanese* Hekiganroku*), or* Blue Cliff Record, *case 89: A Zen student asked his brother, "What does the Bodhisattva of Universal Compassion use so many hands and eyes for?" His brother said, "It's like someone reaching back groping for a pillow in the middle of the night." The first student said, "I understand." His brother asked, "How do you understand?" The first student said, "All over the* *body are hands and eyes." His brother said, "You've said quite a bit there, but you've only said eighty percent." The first student asked, "What do you say?" His brother replied, "Throughout the body are hands and eyes." This illustrates the use of the total body as an organ of energy perception, in the words of the sword master, "seeing with the body, hands, and feet."*

Bringing Back the Mind

The sense of this expression is that when you strike a blow with the sword, if you think to yourself that you have scored, then the mind thinking you've scored stops and stays right there. Since your mind does not come back from the blow you've scored, you become careless and get hit by the adversary's *second sword.* Your initiative turns out to be for naught, and you lose by getting hit with a counterblow.

Bringing back the mind means that when you strike a blow, you don't keep your mind on having struck; after striking, bring your mind back and observe your opponent's condition. Once he is struck, an opponent's mood changes; when one gets hit, one becomes resentful and angry. When angered, an adversary becomes vehement; if you are inattentive, you'll be struck by the opponent.

Think of an opponent who's been hit as a raging wild boar. When you are conscious of having struck a blow, you let your mind tarry and become inattentive. You should be aware than an opponent's energy will emerge when he's hit.

An adversary will also be careful of a place where he's already been hit, so if you try to strike again the same way, you'll miss. When you miss, your opponent will counter and hit you.

Bringing back the mind means bringing your mind back to your body, not letting it linger on having struck a blow. The thing is to bring your mind back to observe your opponent's condition.

On the other hand, when you have struck a focused blow, to strike repeatedly, slashing again and again without bringing your mind back, not letting your opponent so much as turn his head, is also a supremely effective state of mind. This is what is meant by the expression *not a hairsbreadth gap*. The idea is to keep slashing without the slightest interval between one sword stroke and the next.

In a Zen dialogue, which is referred to as a religious battlefield, an answer is given to a question without the slightest gap. If you delay, you will be overtaken by others. Then it is clear who will win and who will lose.

This is what is meant by leaving no gap, not even so much as could admit a single strand of hair. It refers to the rapidity of the sword in repeated strokes.

Attention is a constant theme in martial arts, and the Zen content is ordinarily focused on cultivating constant presence of mind. The reference to Zen dialogue as religious combat is rare in Chinese tradition; it is more characteristic of Japanese Zen, whose samurai patrons may have pursued Zen discipline for adaptation to martial arts, rather than using their martial arts as a medium for Zen training. The great Chinese Zen master Dahui, who was known for his brilliance, refuted the stereotype of swiftness of wit associated with Zen by citing the case of a famous master known as Five Pecks because it was said he used to take so long to answer a question that five pecks of rice could be cooked in the meantime.

The Sense of Total Removal
The Sense of Emptiness
The Sense of Presenting the Mind

Total removal means completely removing all sickness. *Sickness* here means sickness of mind. The thing is to get rid of all the sickness in the mind in one fell swoop.

The varieties of sickness are indicated elsewhere in this book. The general meaning of sickness is the lingering or tarrying of the mind. In Buddhism this is called fixation, and it is severely rejected. If the mind is fixated on one spot and lingers there, you will miss what you should see and suffer unexpected defeat.

The idea that one should get rid of all these sicknesses in one fell swoop is called *total removal*. The sense is that one should totally remove all sicknesses and not fail to perceive the only one.

Now then, *the only one* refers to emptiness. *Emptiness* is a code word, which has to be taught secretly. *Emptiness* refers to the mind of an adversary. Mind is formless and immaterial; that is why it is empty. To see emptiness, the only one, means to see the minds of adversaries.

Buddhism is a matter of realizing emptiness of mind. Although there are people who preach that mind is empty, it is said that there are few who realize it.

As for presenting the mind, the mind of an adversary is presented in the hands that grip the sword. The thing is to strike the adversary's grip before he even makes a move.

Complete removal is for the purpose of seeing that moment of imminent movement. The point is to get rid of all sicknesses at once, and not fail to see emptiness.

The mind of an adversary is in his hands; it is presented

in his hands. To hit them while they are still is called hitting emptiness. Emptiness does not move; because it has no form, it does not move. To hit emptiness means striking swiftly before movement.

Emptiness is the eye of Buddhism. There is a distinction between false emptiness and real emptiness. False emptiness is a simile for nothingness. Real emptiness is genuine emptiness, which is emptiness of mind. Although the mind is like empty space, being formless, the one mind is the master of the body, so the performance of all actions is in the mind.

The movement and working of the mind is the doing of the mind. When the mind is inactive, it is empty; when emptiness is active, it is mind. Emptiness goes into action, becoming mind and working in the hands and feet. Since you are to hit the adversary's hands holding his sword quickly, before they move, it is said that you should "strike emptiness."

Even though we speak of "presenting the mind," the mind is invisible to the eye. It is called empty because of being invisible, and it is also called empty when it is not moving. Although the mind is presented in the hands gripping the sword, it is invisible to the eye. The point is to strike when the mind is presented in the hands but has not yet moved.

You may suppose that this mind-void is nothing because it is invisible, yet when the mind-void moves, it does all sorts of things. Gripping with the hands, treading with the feet, all possible marvels are products of the action of this emptiness, this mind.

It is hard to actually understand this mind even if you read books; this is a path hard to reach even if you listen to sermons. People who write and people who preach just write and preach based on traditional religious writings and lectures; it is said those who have realized the mind at heart are rare.

Since all human actions, even marvels, are doings of the mind, this mind is also in the universe. We call this the mind of the universe. When this mind moves, there is thunder and lightning, wind and rain; it does things like create unseasonable cloud formations and cause hail to rain in midsummer, producing ill effects on humanity.

Thus, in the context of the universe, emptiness is the master of the universe; and in the context of the human body, it is the master of the human body. When dancing, it is the master of dance; when acting, it is the master of drama. When using martial arts, it is the master of martial arts. When shooting a gun, it is the master of the gun; when shooting a bow, it is master of the bow. When riding, it is the master of the horse. If there is a personal warp in the master, one cannot ride a horse or hit the mark with a bow or a gun.

When the mind has found its proper place and position in the body and is settled where it ought to be, one is free in all paths. It is important to find this mind and understand it.

People all think they have perceived and opened up their own minds and are able to employ their own minds usefully, but it is said that very few people have actually found this mind for sure. The signs that they have not attained realization will be evident in their persons, visible to all who have the perception to see.

When people are awakened, everything they do, all their personal conduct, will be straightforward. If they are not straightforward, they can hardly be called enlightened people. The straightforward mind is called the original mind, or the mind of the Way. The warped, polluted mind is called the false or errant mind, or the human mentality.

People who have actually realized their own original mind, and whose actions accord with that mind, are a fascinating phenomenon. I do not speak such words from my own understanding. Although I speak like this, it is hard for me to be direct and straightforward in mind and to behave in a manner consistent with a straightforward mind. I write of it, nevertheless, because it is the Way.

Even so, technique cannot be perfected in martial arts as long as your mind is not straightforward and your body, hands, and feet are not in accord. Even if our everyday behavior is not in accord with the Way, in the path of martial arts this attainment of the Way is imperative.

Even if you do not stray from this mind in any of your activities and accord with this mind in particular arts, it does not work when you try to apply it elsewhere. One who knows everything and can do everything is called an adept. Those who master one art or one craft are called masters of their particular way, but this is not to be called adepthood.

> *Emptiness is central to mainstream Buddhism, but its interpretation and application can be problematic. According to the* Precious Lineage Treatise, *novices tend to have three wrong ideas of emptiness: that emptiness is the result of annihilation, that there is emptiness outside of matter, or that emptiness exists of itself. Nagarjuna, the great Buddhist writer most famed for his work on emptiness, wrote that emptiness is departure from all views, while those who adopt emptiness as a view are incurable.*

> *In Zen, emptiness is understood experientially. The Pan-Buddhist classic* The Flower Ornament Scripture *says, "If you want to know the realm of the enlightened, make your mind as clear as space. Detach from subjective imaginings, and from all fixations, making your mind unimpeded wherever it goes." This is the basis of the mental freedom and agility extolled by the sword master.*

Chinese Chan master Dahui, whose teachings were very influential in late medieval Japan, commented on this passage of scripture, "Make your mind as wide open as cosmic space; detach from conceptual fixations, and false ideas and imaginings will also be like empty space. Then this effortless subtle mind will naturally be unobstructed wherever it goes."

Dahui also said, "In Chan terminology, 'mindlessness' does not mean insensitivity or ignorance. It means that the mind is stable and does not get stirred up by the situations and circumstances you encounter. It means that the mind does not fixate on anything, is clear in all situations, unhindered and unpolluted, not dwelling on anything, even nondefilement."

In the context of martial arts, the mysterious sword or hidden reserve is called emptiness because it exists in a state of potential and only becomes manifest relative to conditions. The mind or intent that is the vanguard of the mysterious sword is even more recondite; it is called emptiness because it is imperceptible yet responds to potential.

True and False Mind

There is a poem that says,

"It is the mind
That is the mind
Confusing the mind.
Don't leave the mind,
O mind,
To the mind."

In the first line, *the mind* refers to the false mind, which is a bad state of mind. It confuses our original mind.

In the second line, *the mind* refers to the false mind.

In the third line, *the mind* refers to the original mind that the false mind confuses.

In the fourth line, *the mind* refers to the original mind.

In the fifth line, *the mind* refers to the original mind.

In the sixth line, *the mind* refers to the false mind.

This poem expresses the true and the false. There are two minds, the original mind and the false mind. If you find the original mind and act in accord, all things are straightforward. When this original mind is warped and polluted by the obscurity of the false mind covering it up, all actions are thereby warped and polluted.

The original mind and the false mind are not two separate entities, like something white and something black. The original mind is the *original face,* which is there before our parents give birth to us. Having no form, it is not born and does not perish.

What is produced by our parents is the physical body. Since the mind is formless and immaterial, we cannot say our parents have given birth to it. It is inherently there in the body when people are born.

We understand Zen to be a teaching that communicates this mind. There is also imitation Zen. A lot of people say similar things that are not really the right path, so people who are supposedly Zennists are not all the same.

When we speak of the false mind, this refers to the energy of the blood, which is personal and subjective. Blood-energy is the action of blood; when blood rises, the color of the face changes and one becomes angry.

When people despise what we love, we become angry and resentful. But if others despise what we despise the way we do, we enjoy this and twist wrong into right.

When people are given valuables, they receive them with delight. They break into smiles, and blood-energy produces a glow in their faces. Then they take what is wrong to be right.

These are all states of mind that come from the energy in the blood in the body, from this physical body, when dealing with temporal situations. These states of mind are referred to as the "false mind."

When this false mind is aroused, the original mind is concealed, becoming a false mind, so only bad things emerge. Therefore enlightened people are honorable because they reduce the false mind by means of the original mind. In unenlightened people, the original mind is hidden while the false mind is powerful; so they act crookedly and get a sullied reputation.

Although the poem quoted above is nothing special, it expresses the distinction between the false and true quite well. Whatever the false mind does is wrong. If this wrong mind emerges, you will lose at martial arts too—you won't hit the target with bow and arrow, you'll miss the mark with a gun, you will not even be able to ride a horse. If you performed in a drama or a dance in this state, it would be unpleasant to watch and listen. Mistakes will also appear in what you say. Everything will be off.

If you accord with the original mind, however, everything you do will be fine.

People contrive artifices claiming they're not faking. Because that is the false mind, its contrivance is already evident. When the heart is true, people who hear you eventually realize it without any justification. The original mind needs no justification.

The false mind is sickness of mind. Getting rid of this false mind is called getting rid of sickness. Rid of this sickness, the mind is sound. This sound mind is called the original mind. If you accord with the original mind, you will excel in martial arts. This principle is relevant to everything, without exception.

Zen is a transcendental teaching, but Zen realization also enhances experience and action in the world because it clarifies and liberates the mind. The reputation Zen thus acquired for improving performance of the arts, however, came to be commercialized by a certain class of followers, in Zen terms a kind of collective false mind, described by Zen master Man-an, a contemporary of the sword master Yagyu, in these terms:

"Even those who are supposedly Zen teachers have not cut off their mental routines and have not arrived at the intent and expression of Zen. Making their living on hallucinations and altered states, they violate the rules of conduct without fear of the consequences. Neglecting the unified work on the Way that includes reading scriptures, bowing to Buddhas, and simply sitting, they reject the refinement and development process that includes sweeping, drawing water, gathering firewood, and preparing meals. The Zen monasteries are like general stores at the crossroads, dealing in poetry and song, prose and verse, calligraphy and painting, calculating, stamps, tea, incenses, medicine, divination, and all sorts of other arts. They engage in trade and commerce whenever the opportunity or demand arises. Can you call this means of dealing with the masses for the sake of the people?"

Book 3

NO SWORD

~

Being swordless does not necessarily mean that you have to take someone's sword. Nor does it mean making a show of sword-snatching for the sake of your reputation. It is the swordless art of not getting killed when you have no sword. The basic intention is nothing like deliberately setting out to snatch a sword.

It is not a matter of insistently trying to wrest away what is being kept from your grasp. Not grasping what is being deliberately kept from your grasp is also swordlessness.

Someone who is intent on not having his sword taken away forgets what he's opposed to and just tries to avoid having his sword taken away. He will therefore be unable to kill anyone. Not being killed oneself is considered a victory.

The principle is not to make an art of taking away other's swords. It is learning to avoid being cut down by others when you have no sword yourself.

Swordlessness is not the art of taking another's sword. It is for the purpose of using all implements freely. If you can even take away another's sword when you're unarmed and make it your own, then what will not be useful in your hands? Even with only a folding fan you can still prevail over someone with a sword. This is the aim of swordlessness.

Suppose you're walking along with a bamboo cane when someone draws a long sword and attacks you. If you take his sword away, you win, even though you respond with only a cane. Or, if you don't take his sword away, you win if you thwart him so that he can't cut you down. This attitude should be regarded as the basic idea of swordlessness.

Swordlessness is not for the purpose of taking swords, nor for killing people. When an enemy insistently tries to kill you, that is when you should take his sword. The taking itself is not the original intention at the outset. It is for the purpose of attaining an effective understanding of the margin of safety. This means gauging the distance between you and an enemy at which his sword won't reach you.

If you know the distance at which you're out of range, you're not fearful of an opponent's striking sword. When your body is exposed to attack, then you actively think about this exposure. As for swordlessness, as long as you are out of range of another's sword you can't take it away. You have to expose yourself to being killed in order to take a sword away.

Swordlessness is the calculation by which others may have swords but you engage them using your hands as your instruments. Since swords are longer than arms, you have to get close to an adversary, within killing range, in order to be successful at this.

It is necessary to distinguish the interplay of your opponent's sword and your hands. Then when your adversary's sword overshoots your body, you get underneath the hilt of the sword, aiming to arrest the sword.

When the time comes, don't freeze into a fixed pattern. In any event, you can't take an opponent's sword away unless you keep close.

Swordlessness is the foremost secret of this school. Physical posture, positioning of the sword, taking a stand, distance, movement, contrivance, sticking, attacking, appearance and intention—all come from swordless calculation, so this is the essential eye.

Swordless calculation is the minimum margin of safety from which it is also possible to slip into striking distance of the enemy. All of the items enumerated, from posture to tactics, are based on continual calculation of the distance at which defense and offense are both effective. This calculation is based on swordlessness because the margin of safety is absolutely critical without a weapon, which thus defines the inner boundary of defense; while the proximity needed to counter with bare hands is less than what would be required with a weapon, thus defining the outer limit or maximum distance within which offense can be effective.

Great Potential and Great Function

Everything has body and function. If there is a body, it has function. For example, a bow is a body, while drawing, shooting, and hitting the target are functions of a bow. A lamp is a body, light is its function. Water is a body, moisture is a function of water. An apricot tree is a body, fragrance and color are functions. A sword is a body, cutting and stabbing are functions.

So potential is the body, while the existence of various capabilities, manifesting outwardly from the potential, is called function. Because an apricot tree has a body, flowers blossom from the body, emanating color and scent. In the same way, function resides within potential and works outside; sticking, attacking, appearance and intention, aggressive and passive modes, the casting of various impressions, and so on, manifest external action because there is potential at the ready within. These are called function.

Great is a laudatory expression. When we say *Great Spirit, Great Incarnation,* and *Great Saint,* the word *great* is an expression of praise. Great function appears because of great potential. When Zen monks are able to use their bodies freely and independently, harmonizing with truth and communing with truth whatever they say and do, this is called great spiritual power, or great function of great potential.

Spiritual powers and miraculous manifestations are not wonders produced by ghosts or spirits from outer space; these terms refer to working freely and independently whatever you do. All the many sword positions, appearances concealing intentions, deceptions, use of implements, leaping up and leaping down, grabbing a blade, kicking someone down—all sorts of actions—are called great function when you attain independence beyond what you have learned. Unless you always have the potential there within, great function will not appear.

Even when you are sitting indoors, first look up, then look left and right, to see if there is anything that might happen to fall from above. When seated by a door or screen, take note of whether it might not fall over. If you happen to be in attendance near nobles of high rank, be aware of whether something unexpected might happen. Even when you are going in and out a door, don't neglect attention to the going out and going in, always keeping aware. These are all examples of potential.

Because this potential is always there within, when it is natural, an extraordinary speed occurs; this is called great function. When potential is unripe, function does not become manifest. In all paths, when concentration builds up and exercise is repeated, potential matures and great function emerges.

When potential freezes, stiffens up, and remains inflexible, it is not functional. When it matures, it expands throughout the body, so that great function emerges through the hands and feet, eyes and ears.

When you meet people with this great potential and great function, martial arts using only what you have learned will not even enable you to raise a hand. Once you're glared at by the eyes of someone with the great potential, you'll be so captivated by the look you'll forget to draw your sword, just standing there doing nothing.

If you delay for even the time it takes to blink an eye, you'll have lost already. When a cat glares at it, a mouse falls down from the ceiling; captivated by the look in the cat's eyes, the mouse falls, forgetting even to run. Encountering someone with the great potential is like a mouse encountering a cat.

There is a Zen saying, "When the great function appears, it does not keep to guidelines." This means that people with the great potential and great function are not at all constrained by learning or rules. In all fields of endeavor, there are things to learn and there are rules. People who have attained supreme mastery are beyond them; they act freely and independently. To act independently, outside of rules, is called personifying great potential and great function.

Potential means to be thinking attentively of everything. So when that intently thought potential becomes stiff and frozen and hard, then you are entangled by potential and thus are not free. This is because the potential is immature. If you build up effective exercise, the potential will mature, expanding throughout the body, working freely. This is called the great function.

Potential is energy. It is called potential according to the situation. Mind is the inside, energy is the entrance. Since the mind is master of the whole body, it should be understood as that which resides within; energy is at the door, working outside for the mind, its master.

The division of mind into good and bad comes from this potential, as it goes out from states of potential to good and to bad. Energy that is kept watchfully at the door is called potential. When people open a door and go outside, whether they do good, do evil, or even work marvels, is due to the ideas in their minds before opening the door.

Therefore this potential is something very important. If this potential is working, it emerges outside and the great function manifests.

In any case, if you understand it as energy, you will not be off. It is called differently according to where it is.

Even so, just because we speak of the inside and the entrance, there are no fixed definitions of inside and entrance somewhere in the body. We speak of inside and entrance as metaphors. For example, when people speak, the beginning of their speech could be called the entrance, while the end could be called the inside. There are no specific locations of inside and entrance in the words themselves.

The science of energy comes from Taoism, which is the true progenitor of the martial arts of Asia. Warning that guarding the door does not mean focusing on a particular place in the body is also found in Taoist lore. A common Taoist practice involves focusing attention on a system of sensitive regions in the body, but this practice has drawbacks, and it is disavowed in some schools. The habit of focusing attention in the lower abdomen is originally part of this system, but isolated from the totality it tends to have negative side effects, such as the stagnation of energy. Just as Munenori Yagyu repeatedly warns of the deadly danger of attention fixation in martial arts, latter-day Taoist master Liu

I-ming warned of the neurophysiological dangers of attention fixation:

"I have seen many cases of people suffering from brain leakage through fixation of attention on points in their heads. Those who keep attention fixed on points in their lower torso often suffer leakage from below. Those who keep their attention fixed on the solar plexus area often get bloated. Those who keep their attention fixed on the forehead lose their eyesight. Those who try to keep a blank mind develop symptoms of epilepsy.

"Wishing to seek long life, instead they hasten death. It is a pity they don't know the primal, open, immaterial energy that enfolds the universe and produces and develops all beings. It is so great that it has no outside, so fine it has no inside. Release it, and it fills the universe; wrap it up, and it withdraws into storage in secrecy. It can only be known, not spoken; it can only be nurtured, not fixed upon."

Mind and Objects

A verse by Reverend Manora says, "Mind turns along with myriad situations; its turning point is truly recondite." This verse refers to a Zen secret; I cite it here because this idea is quintessential to martial arts. People who don't study Zen will find it quite hard to comprehend.

In the context of martial arts, *myriad situations* mean all the actions of adversaries; the mind turns with each and every action. For example, when an opponent raises his sword, your mind turns to the sword. If he whirls to the right, your mind turns to the right; if he whirls to the left, your mind turns to the left. This is called "turning along with myriad situations."

As for *"the turning point is truly recondite,"* this is the eye of martial arts. When the mind does not leave any traces in any particular place, but turns to what lies ahead, with the past dying out like the wake of a boat, not lingering at all, this should be understood as the turning point being truly recondite.

To be recondite is to be subtle and imperceptible. This means the mind doesn't linger on any particular point. If your mind stops and stays somewhere, you will be defeated in martial arts. If you linger where you turn, you will be crushed.

Since the mind has no form or shape, it is basically invisible; but when it fixates and lingers, the mind is visible as such in that condition. It is like raw silk—dye it red and it becomes red; dye it violet and it becomes violet. The human mind also manifests visibly when it is attracted and fixated by things. If you are attracted to boys, eventually people will notice. When the thought is within, the impression appears outwardly.

When you are watching an opponent's moves carefully, if you let your mind linger there, you will lose at martial arts. The verse cited above is quoted to illustrate this point, not to let the mind linger. I omit the last two lines of the verse. For Zen study, it is necessary to know the whole verse; in martial arts, the first two are enough.

Reverend Manora is reckoned as the twenty-second patriarch of Zen Buddhism in India. The last two lines of the verse, omitted by the sword master as mentioned, run, "When you recognize nature and accord with its flow, there is no more elation or depression." The famous Japanese psychiatrist Morita Masatake, originator of the Morita method of psychotherapy, often cited this verse in his work. The sword master's omission of the last two lines shows that Zen and martial arts do not coincide in every respect, as he himself acknowledges. There is the possibility for interpretation and application of the crossroads of these paths in a manner that is more mechanical than spiritual, as the sword master illustrates in the next section.

Martial Arts and Buddhism

There are many things in martial arts that accord with Buddhism and correspond to Zen. In particular, there is repudiation of attachment and avoidance of lingering on anything. This is the most urgent point. Not lingering is considered quintessential.

A courtesan wrote this poem in response to one by the Buddhist priest Saigyo:

"If you ask as a leaver of home,

I simply think you should

Not let your mind linger

On a temporary dwelling."

In martial arts we should savor the last lines deeply, and see if we are not like this. No matter what kind of secret transmission you obtain and what move you employ, if your mind lingers on that move you will have lost in martial arts.

It is essential to practice an attitude of not dwelling on anything, be it the actions of an opponent, your own skills, or slashing and stabbing.

Saigyo (1118–1190) was a famous priest-poet. Originally a soldier, he abandoned the world at the age of twenty-three to become a Buddhist priest. He spent most of his life traveling. The courtesan's poem cited here comes from a well-known incident on one of his journeys, when he sought lodging one night.

Nonattachment is the first phase of Zen; not dwelling on nonattachment is the second phase; not making an understanding of not dwelling is the third phase. In poetic terms, these phases are also referred to as "the bird's path" (of nonattachment), "the mystic path" (of not even dwelling in nonattachment,) and "going to town with open arms" (not making an understanding of not dwelling).

The difference between the first two phases is exemplified in a Zen koan, wherein someone asked a Zen master, "When not a single thing is brought, then what?" The master said, "Put it down." The questioner asked, "If I don't bring a single thing, what should I put down?" The master said, "Then carry it out."

A classical commentary on this koan borrows the metaphor of contest and illustrates its application to martial arts:

"Not prepared for meticulous action, he loses to the first to move —

"Realizing the coarseness of his own mind, he's embarrassed at bumping his head.

"By the time the game's over, the ax handle's rotted at his side;

"Clean and purify the ordinary bones to play with the immortals."

Yes and No

Master Longji said to a group, "The pillar of affirmation does not see the pillar. The pillar of denial does not see the pillar. Having gotten rid of affirmation and denial altogether, attain understanding within affirmation and denial." This saying is supposed to be applied to all arts. A certain teacher told it to me, and I thought of its application to martial arts, so I record it here.

As for "the pillar of affirmation" and "the pillar of denial," this means that judgments of right and wrong, good and bad, stand firmly in the heart, affirmation and denial being like pillars standing. Even keeping something right in mind will suddenly become onerous; if it is something wrong, it will be even more onerous. Therefore the saying has it that you do not see the pillars. This means that you should not look at the pillars of affirmation and denial.

These judgments of affirmation and denial, good and bad, are sicknesses of the mind. As long as these sicknesses do not leave the mind, whatever you do is not good. Therefore the saying goes that we should attain understanding within affirmation and denial after having gotten rid of affirmation and denial. This means that after having detached from affirmation and denial, you should then mix in with affirmation and denial, rising from the midst of affirmation and denial to the supreme state.

The eye detached from affirmation and denial is truly hard to attain, even if you have understood Buddhism.

The problem of reconciling morality and transcendence often plagued Buddhist schools teaching emptiness. It was even more difficult for samurai bound hand and foot to the authority of personal masters. Eminent Chinese Chan master Baizhang (Hyakujo), ancestor of the Linji (Rinzai) school of Zen, explained that the full integration of consciousness is a matter of order and balance in the process of refinement:

"The words of the teachings all have three successive steps; the elementary, intermediate, and final good. At first it is just necessary to teach people to develop a good mind. In the intermediate stage, they break through the good mind. The last stage is finally called really good. . . . If, however, you teach only one stage, you will cause people to go to hell. If all three stages are taught at once, they'll go to hell on their own. This is not the work of a real teacher."

He also explained the sense of good in this Zen context,

"Realizing that the present mirroring awareness is your own Buddha is the elementary good. Not to keep dwelling in the immediate mirroring awareness is the intermediate good. Not to make an understanding of nondwelling either is the final good."

Truth and Untruth

"Even truth is to be relinquished; how much more untruth." In this passage, *truth* means really true teaching. Even really true teaching should not be kept in mind once you have become completely enlightened. Thus "even truth is to be relinquished."

After you have realized true teaching, if you keep it in your heart, it pollutes your heart; how much more does untruth! Since even truth is to be relinquished, how much more so if it is untruth—this should not be kept in your heart. That is what this passage says.

> *This passage comes from the* Diamond Cutter Scripture, *which was commonly recited in Zen schools. It is a summary of the Buddhist prajnaparamita teaching, which emphasizes transcending doctrine and method.*

Having seen all true principles, do not keep any of them in your chest. Let go of them cleanly, making your heart empty and open, and do what you do in an ordinary and unconcerned state of mind.

You can hardly be called a master of martial arts unless you reach this stage.

I speak of martial arts because military science is my family business, but this principle is not to be limited to martial arts. All arts and sciences, and all walks of life, are like this. When you employ martial arts, unless you get rid of the idea of martial arts, it is a sickness. When you shoot, unless you get rid of the idea of shooting, it is the sickness of archery.

If you just duel and shoot with a normal mind, you should have no trouble with the bow, and you should be able to wield a sword freely. The normal mind, not upset by anything, is good for everything. If you lose the normal mind, your voice will quiver whatever you try to say. If you lose the normal mind, your hand will quiver if you try to write something in front of others.

The normal mind keeps nothing in the heart, but lightly relinquishes the past, so that the heart is empty and therefore is the normal mind. People who read Confucian books, failing to understand this principle of emptying the mind, get stuck on the notion of seriousness. Seriousness is not the ultimate realization, but training in the first couple of steps.

In neo-Confucian meditation, "seriousness" refers to keeping the mind on one point. Insofar as it represents a means rather than an end, striving rather than spontaneity, this practice of "seriousness" does not reach the level of mastery of prajnaparamita or Zen. Neo-Confucianism was an important element of feudal Japanese education, and as such was incorporated into contemporary political science as well as the warrior code of Bushido. Yagyu's repeated references to neo-Confucian theory and practice reflect this aspect of the background training of warriors of his time. His insistence on the superiority of Zen was not politically correct, and not a reflection of religious dogma or prejudice, but based on experiential practicality of the warrior's way.

THE INSCRUTABLE SUBTLETY OF IMMOVABLE WISDOM

~~~

By Zen Master Takuan (1573-1645)

The Affliction of Ignorant States of Fixation

Ignorance is written with characters meaning "no enlightenment" and refers to confusion. A *state of fixation* is written with characters meaning a "state of lingering" and refers to the fifty-two stages of Buddhist practice. Within these fifty-two stages, wherever the mind lingers is called a state of fixation. *Fixation* means lingering, and *lingering* means keeping the mind on something, whatever it may be.

> *The fifty-two stages of Buddhist practice are detailed in the* Flower Ornament Scripture. *Zen usage of scriptures and systems is concerned with essence rather than form, so doctrine and practice are considered expedients to be ultimately transcended. Abstract fixations are considered as inhibiting as concrete fixations, and Zen teachings demonstrate a great deal of effort to overcome the tendency to become attached to mental objects. The practical expedients for Zen awakening are likened to medicine, which is used to cure illness and not to be taken once health is restored. Similarly, in the Zen approach to martial arts, learning postures, moves, and techniques is a matter of expediency, for the master of martial arts must be able*

to respond to situations instantly as they unfold, without stopping to think about postures, moves, and techniques.

To express this in terms of your martial art, the moment you see an opponent come with a cutting stroke, if you think of parrying it right then and there, your mind lingers on the opponent's sword that way, so you fail to act in time; thus you get killed by the opponent. This is called lingering.

The cognitive mind conceives constants in the flux of phenomena and flow of events, but in the context of combat, where instantaneous adaptation to the unexpected is essential, this "freeze frame" function of cognition, otherwise necessary for ordinary life, becomes a fatal handicap. As a Zen saying describes it, "As soon as you call it thus and so, it has already changed." Therefore the moment-to-moment presence of mind produced by Zen training is valued by martial artists for overcoming internal complications and diversions caused by entanglement in conceptualization.

If you don't keep your mind on the sword even as you see it, and don't think about striking according to the rhythm of the opponent's sword, but move right in to take his sword the moment you see the sword raised, without keeping your mind on it at all, you can snatch away the sword about to kill you and turn it into a sword to kill your opponent instead. In Zen this is called "snatching the lance and turning it around to stab the other." This means taking your opponent's sword and killing him with it. This is what you yourself call "no sword."

In Zen technical literature, the expression "snatching the lance and turning it around to stab the other" is commonly applied to descriptions of interactive teaching wherein a question is posed to elicit a response indicative of a state of mind so that this state of mind can be addressed from a Zen point of view and its fixation dispelled. In terms of martial arts this is the equivalent of feinting in order to observe an opponent's pattern of reaction. When the tables are turned, so that a questioner is cornered with his own question, like an attacker being counterattacked with his own weapon, this is called "snatching the lance and turning it around to stab the other." Whether in Zen dialogue or in a sword duel, the essential technique is to avoid having attention captured by the external form of an approach or attack, instead acting directly on its intention and taking command of its energetic charge.

Whether an opponent attacks or you attack, if you fix your mind on the attacker, the attacking sword, the pace or the rhythm, even for a moment, your own actions will be delayed, and you'll be killed.

The Diamond Cutter Scripture *says, "Activate the mind without dwelling anywhere." According to legend, Huineng, the illustrious sixth grand master of Chinese Zen was suddenly enlightened on hearing this phrase. It has become a watchword of Zen practice ever since.*

While your attention will be taken by the enemy if you put your mind on the enemy's physical presence, you shouldn't put your mind on yourself either. Even if you keep your mind focused on your own body, that should be done only as a beginner in training; your attention will be taken by the sword. If you set your mind on the rhythm, your attention will be taken by the rhythm. If you set your mind on your own sword, your attention will be taken by your sword. In any of these cases, your mind lingers, and you become an empty shell.

> *Zen master Hui-neng said, "When you do not dwell on the inward or the outward, coming and going freely, you are able to eliminate the clinging mentality and penetrate without obstruction."*

You should be aware of this. I speak in terms of analogy to Buddhism. Buddhism refers to the fixated mind as confusion, so it is called the affliction of ignorant fixation.

> *Zen master Hui-neng said, "If you open to understanding of the teaching of immediacy, you do not cultivate practice grasping externals; you simply activate accurate perception at all times in your own mind, so afflictions and passions can never influence you." This fluid presence of mind is critical to the martial artist in the midst of action, when any lapse of attention to the immediate moment opens a fatal gap in defense.*

The Immovable Wisdom of the Buddhas

Immovable does not mean inanimate; when the mind doesn't linger at all as it moves in any direction desired—left, right, all around, in all directions—that is called immovable wisdom.

> *Immovability does not mean immobility, but imperturbability. This implies that the attention is diverted and the mind not disarrayed by external phenomena or internal states. In Zen teaching this is carefully distinguished from mental stasis, as explained by master Hakuin:*
>
> *"If potential does not leave its state, it falls into an ocean of poison. This is what Buddha called the great folly of*

> *grasping realization in the absolute state. Even if you have clarified true cognition of equality, you cannot activate subtle observing cognition seeing all things without impediment. Therefore, although you may be perfectly clear inside and out as long as you are hidden away in an unfrequented place where there is absolute quiet and nothing to do, yet as soon as perception touches upon different worldly situations, with all their clamor and emotion, you are powerless, beset by many miseries."*

The Immovable Luminary King holds a sword in his right hand and a rope in his left hand; gritting his teeth, eyes glaring, he stands thus ready to vanquish demons who would interfere with Buddhism. He is not hidden in any land in any world. He appears to people as a protector of Buddhism, while in substance he is an embodiment of this immutable wisdom.

> *The Immovable Luminary King, in Japanese Fudo Myo-o, is a figure from Buddhist iconography, normally depicted standing guard outside monastery gates. The luminary kings are conceived of as demons converted to become protectors of religion, in this sense representing anger directed toward overcoming evil. Thus while the Immovable Luminary King symbolizes the imperturbable attitude of the Zen warrior, this imagery is also used as an expression of an underlying moral rationale for the way of the samurai.*

Wholly ordinary people avoid opposing Buddhism out of fear, but those who are near enlightenment understand that he represents immovable wisdom. If you clear away all confusion and thus clarify immovable wisdom, then you yourself are the Immovable Luminary King; so the Immovable

Luminary King is there to inform you that even demons will not be allowed to molest people who can put this state of mind into effect.

> *Zen teaching refers to this as a state of mind that "wind cannot penetrate, water cannot wet, fire cannot burn," a state where "demons secretly spying can find no way to see, deities offering flowers cannot discover a trail."*

Therefore, the so-called Immovable Luminary King refers to the state when a person's whole mind is immovable. It is a matter of not letting oneself get upset. Not being upset is a matter of not lingering over anything. Seeing things at once without keeping your mind on them is called being unmoved.

> *Zen master Chinul wrote, "If you conceive aversion or attraction, this will cause you to grasp those repulsive or attractive objects. If the mind is not aroused, however, then it is unobstructed."*

The reason for this is that when the mind lingers on things, all sorts of thoughts come to mind, so all sorts of movement take place in your heart. When it stops, the stationary mind does not stir even in movement.

> *Chinul wrote, "When the mind is aroused and exhausted along with inconstant objects, the mind on inconstant objects is opposite to the normal constant true mind."*

For example, suppose ten people attack you with swords, one after another. If you parry each sword without keeping your mind on it afterward, leaving behind one to take on another, your action will not fail to deal with all ten. Even though your mind acts ten times for ten people, if you don't fix your mind on any one of them, the act of taking them on one after another will not fail. Then again, if your mind lingers in the presence of one of them, even though you may parry one man's striking sword, you will fail to act in time when the next one attacks.

> *Zen master Shoju Rojin was once confronted by samurai disciples who asserted that his realization might be superior to theirs in the abstract but theirs was superior to his in concrete application. The Zen master responded by challenging them to a duel, facing their swords with only an iron-clad fan, parrying every blow. Stymied, the humbled samurai asked about his technique. The Zen master replied that he had no technique but clarity of the enlightened eye.*

The reason why Kannon of the Thousand Hands needs a thousand hands is that if the mind is fixed on the hand holding the bow, then the other nine hundred and ninety-nine hands will be useless. By not keeping the mind on any one place, all the hands become useful. Why would Kannon need a thousand hands on one body? This image was created to show people that once immovable wisdom is activated, even if one has a thousand hands they are all useful.

> *Kannon is a Japanese version of the name of Avalokitesvara, one of the most important figures of mainstream Buddhist iconography, representing the saving power of compassion. Because compassion implies versatility and adaptability, Kannon is portrayed in many forms. The form referred to as Kannon of the Thousand Hands has a halo of hands holding all sorts of implements, representing the skillfulness of a Buddhist bodhisattva and the panoply of ways and means of educating, enlightening, and liberating people.*

If you look at a tree and see only one of its red leaves, you don't see the rest of the foliage. If you look at the tree casually without setting your mind on one leaf, you see all the foliage. If your mind is taken up by one leaf, then you don't see the rest of the leaves, but if you don't set your mind on one, then you can see all hundred thousand of them. One who understands this becomes Kannon of the Thousand Hands and Thousand Eyes.

> *The phenomenon of being "unable to see the forest for the trees" reflects the same selective feature of brain function. While this proverb is commonly used in reference to a conceptual appreciation of a situation, in Zen and martial arts it is preeminently perceptual. Zen master Bunan taught, "There is no special principle in the study of the way—it's only necessary to perceive directly."*

Nonetheless, wholly ordinary people simply believe there are a thousand hands and a thousand eyes on one body, regarding this as marvelous. Then again, dilettantes with superficial knowledge repudiate it as nonsense — what is the purpose of having a thousand eyes on one body? Now when you know a little better, you respect the principle; it is neither what ordinary people believe nor what they repudiate — it is a matter of Buddhist teaching illustrating a principle through an object.

> *Confusion of literal and symbolic understanding is an endemic problem in organized religion, when the original inspiration has been replaced by imitation. For this reason, the revelation of symbolic meaning in scripture, the restoration of mythology to psychology, was one of the specialties of the original teachings of Zen. This internalization of meaning is key to Zen expression in all the arts.*

All the various Ways are like this; especially, it seems, the Way of the Spirits. It is naïve to think of it literally, yet it is wrong to repudiate it; there is a principle contained therein. Even though the various Ways differ, ultimately they have a certain point.

In the context of Japanese culture, the "Way of the Spirits" refers to Shinto. This is a general term, however, and the religious phenomena to which it refers are also found in Korean, Chinese, Mongolian, Tibetan, and other cultures in which Buddhism operated. The careful distinction made here between naïve literalism and abstract symbolism is characteristic of original Zen. Although mythology was retrieved from fantasy and restored to practical use on the human plane this way, in time memories of events and persons on the human plane also regressed into mythology.

Now then, you should be aware that having cultivated practice from the state of the beginner's mind, when you pass the stage of immovable wisdom, you must return to the state of the beginner.

The "state of the beginner" here refers to innocence, not ineptness. The principle, applied to all arts approached in a Zen manner, is that method is eventually to be transcended once the spirit of an art is embodied. The scriptural image commonly used to illustrate this is that of a raft used to cross a river; once the other shore is reached, the raft is abandoned and the traveler goes on unencumbered. In martial arts, this level of internalization is what makes it possible to apply learning freely to real-life situations, to transcend conscious contrivance and arrive at spontaneity.

This may be expressed in terms of your martial art. A beginner knows nothing about posture or position of the sword, so there is no dwelling on body or mind; if someone attacks him, he scrambles to deal with it mindlessly. As he learns various things, however — physical posture, how to wield the sword, where to place the mind — his mind dwells on various points; if he tries to strike someone, what with one thing and another, he is exceptionally handicapped.

When he has practiced daily for months and years, finally his posture and way of wielding the sword become mindless, like he was at first when he didn't know anything and there was nothing to it. This is the frame of mind in which the beginning and the end are the same. If you count from one to ten and over again, then one and ten are next to one another. In the musical scale too, when you go from A to G from one octave to the next, then A and G are next to one another; the lowest and the highest come to resemble each other.

> *The return to natural unself-conscious simplicity is a hallmark of the teaching of Taoism, the precursor of Zen.* Liezi, *a Taoist classic, says:*
>
> *"Don't dwell on yourself and things will be clear. Like water in movement, like a mirror in stillness, like an echo in response, the Way is thus in harmony with things.*
>
> *"Beings deviate from the Way on their own; the Way does not deviate from beings. Those who harmonize with the Way don't even need their ears or eyes, don't use their strength or their mind. If you want to harmonize with the Way but seek it by means of looking and listening and formal knowledge, you'll never attain it.*

"When you look it lies ahead, but suddenly it's behind; try to use it and it fills the universe, try to dismiss it and no one knows where it is. The mindful cannot alienate it, the mindless cannot approach it; the only ones who attain it realize it silently and actualize it naturally. Knowledge without subjectivity, capability without artifice — these are true knowledge and true capability."

Similarly, when you master Buddhism, you become like someone who knows nothing of Buddha or Dharma, with no perceptible embellishment. Therefore the affliction of ignorance in the beginning state and the immovable wisdom in the end become one; intellectualism disappears and you settle down in a state where there is no mind and no thought. Wit doesn't come out in ignorant ordinary people because they don't have any; a fully developed wit doesn't come out at all, on the other hand, because it has already gone underground. It is because of immature dilettantism that wit comes to mind, silly and ridiculous. Indeed, you must think the manners of today's clergy quite ridiculous. It is shameful.

Some Zen teachings use expressions such as "being like a complete ignoramus" to refer to transcending intellectualism. The uncomplimentary reference to contemporary clergy here alludes to those who took such teachings too literally.

There is abstract practice and concrete practice. The abstract principle is as I have explained; ultimately you don't bother with anything — it's just a matter of relinquishing the mind, as I have written. Nevertheless, if you do not do concrete practice, and just keep principles in mind, then neither your body nor your hands will work.

In terms of your martial art, concrete practice refers to the five postures and the various other things you have to learn. Even if you know the principles, you have to be able to apply them freely in fact. Yet you cannot master the postures and swordplay if you are ignorant of the ultimate point of the principles. The nonduality of fact and principle, the concrete and the abstract, must be like the wheels of a chariot.

> *The illusion of secondhand knowledge and the impor-*
> *tance of actual practice are emphasized in the Zen*
> *proverb, "No one asks about the sweating horses of the*
> *past—they all want to talk about the achievement that*
> *crowns the age."*

Not a Hairsbreadth Gap

This can be expressed by analogy with your martial art. *Gap* means the space between two things, and this expression means that not even a hair can fit in the gap. For example, when you clap your hands, the sound comes forth at once, just like that. The sound comes out with no interval between the clap and the sound, not even so much as a hairsbreadth. The sound does not come out having deliberated for a while after the hands clap—the sound comes out as the hands clap.

If your mind lingers on the sword that someone is striking with, a gap appears, and in that interval your own action is missing. If there is not so much as a hairsbreadth between an opponent's striking sword and your own action, then it is as if your opponent's sword is your own.

This state of mind is found in Zen dialogues. In Buddhism, we don't like to stop and let the mind linger on things. Therefore we call fixation an affliction. We value having no fixated mind at all, flowing freely like a ball on a rushing river, riding the flow even over obstructions.

> *A Zen proverb illustrates this fluidity: "Meeting situations without getting stuck, adepts have the ability to come forth with every move." Zen master Zihu said, "All things are free-flowing, untrammeled—what bondage is there, what entanglement? You create your own difficulty and ease therein. The mind source pervades the ten directions with one continuity; those of the most excellent faculties understand naturally."*

The Capacity to Act in a Flash

This also refers to the aforementioned state of mind. When you strike a flint, a flash appears at once; since the sparks appear the moment you strike the flint, there is no interval or gap. This too refers to the absence of any space in which the mind can linger.

It's wrong to understand this simply in terms of speed. The point is not to let the mind come to a halt on anything. It means that the mind does not come to a halt, even quickly. Once the mind comes to a stop, your mind is taken over by someone else. If you intentionally act quickly, then the mind will still be taken away by the intention of acting quickly.

> *Substitution of speed for spontaneity is a familiar phenomenon in decadent Zen; Takuan's earlier uncomplimentary reference to the exercise of wit alludes to this in the context of Zen dialogue and composition. In martial arts, deliberate speed and spontaneous speed have completely different energetic results. Deliberate speed drains energy, while spontaneous speed conserves energy.*

Deliberate speed narrows attention by focus on intent, while spontaneous speed frees attention by unleashing unmediated response.

A reply to a poem by Saigyo by a prostitute of Eguchi says,

"If you ask about people

Who reject the world,

They're only thinking

Not to let the mind linger

On a temporary dwelling."

You should understand the poem on your own, but you should realize that the thing to understand is just thinking not to let the mind linger, and this is the way to comprehend it.

Saigyo was a monk of the Tendai school of Buddhism, one of the parent schools of Zen. Takuan uses this famous poem to drive home the point that transcendence of objects is not approached by negating objects held in mind, but by ceasing to hold objects in mind.

In the Zen school, you can reply to the question "What is Buddha?" by raising your fist. In reply to the question "What is the ultimate meaning of Buddhism?" you can say, before the questioner has even finished asking, "A plum blossom," or "The cypress tree in the yard." It is not a matter of choosing a felicitous answer, it is valuing the mind that does not linger.

Simple gestures or objects used to answer Zen questions are referred to as points of entry or access, implying that the gesture or object itself is not the answer, but the greater whole of which the gesture or object is a part, including the very experience of being, and the experience of experience itself. Taken out of context, Takuan's presentation here would seem perilously close to approval of the arbitrary answer syndrome characteristic of artificial spontaneity cultivated in imitation Zen cults and denounced by Zen masters. The principle of not lingering, however, is not linear but spatial, a way of seeing part and whole at once. The Zen classic Blue Cliff Record *says, "A device, a perspective, a word, a statement, temporarily intended to provide a point of access, is still gouging a wound in healthy flesh — it can become an object of fixation. The great function appears without abiding by fixed principles, in order that you may realize that there is something transcendental that covers heaven and earth yet cannot be grasped."*

The mind that does not linger is not affected by sense data. The essence of this unaffected mind is celebrated as Spirit, honored as Buddha, and referred to as the Zen mind or the ultimate meaning. What you say after thinking about it may be eloquent, but it is still an affliction of a state of fixation.

When we speak of the capacity to act in a flash, that refers to lightning-like speed. For example, when you call someone by name, an immediate response is called immovable wisdom. When someone is called by name and then wonders what for, the mind subsequently wondering why is afflicted by fixation. The mind that comes to a halt and is stirred and confused by things is that of an ordinary person afflicted by fixation.

Again, answering at once when called is the wisdom of the Buddhas. Buddhas and ordinary people are not two different things; Spirit and humanity are not two different things. Conformity to this mind is called Spirit, and also Buddha. Although there are many Ways, such as the Spirit Way, Poetry, and Confucianism, all of them refer to the illumination of this one mind.

> *While it was normal for Buddhists, particularly Zen Buddhists, to acknowledge the unity of the noumenal ground of all arts, sciences, and religions, in practice the unity of the paths often remained rhetorical. The association of Zen and Confucianism was already established in China before Zen was imported to Japan, but was not much emphasized by Japanese Zen teachers until the seventeenth century, when the military government of Japan sought totalitarian control over every organ of culture. Chinese Confucianism, moreover, was more highly influenced by Zen than was Japanese Confucianism.*

> *The association of Buddhism and mystical Shinto goes back to the earliest centuries of Japanese Buddhist history, but this too only became a standard feature of Japanese Zen Buddhist rhetoric in the seventeenth century. Poetry and Zen intermarried much earlier in Japan, but the vast literary corpus produced by the central Zen establishments, the so-called Five Mountains Literature, was considered sterile by practicing Zen masters and completely ignored by the leaders of the Zen revival of the seventeenth and eighteenth centuries.*

> *The rhetoric Takuan is using, therefore, is not intended to refer to historical phenomena, or to sectarian beliefs,*

but alludes to the critical aim of Zen practice that opens access to the source of all arts and sciences.

As far as the mind can be explained in words, this one mind applies to others and self; good and bad deeds by day and by night come from accumulated habit, alienation and exile depend on personal status and condition, good and evil are both actions of the mind—but no one questions and realizes what this mind is, so everyone is deluded by the mind. It can be affirmed that there are people in the world who don't know the mind, while it seems that those who actually understand it are rarely found. And even if one has understanding and knowledge, they are difficult to put into practice.

Zen master Mazu said, "All kinds of establishments derive from one mind—you may set them up, and you may dismantle them. Both are inconceivable functions."

Being able to explain this one mind is certainly not tantamount to understanding the mind. Even if you explain water as a phenomenon, that does not slake thirst; and even if you talk about fire, your mouth doesn't heat up. You cannot know these things unless you come in contact with actual water and fire. You cannot know just by explaining books. You may talk about food, but that doesn't satisfy hunger. You cannot know just by talk. Even though Buddhism and Confucianism both talk about mind, without corresponding behavior the mind is not clearly known. People don't understand the mind within themselves unless they sincerely examine its fundament and come to realize it.

Zen teachings are for inducing firsthand experience. While many Zen masters were accomplished scholars, none of them claimed to understand Zen through formal learning alone; as a famous saying has it, "a picture of a cake can't satisfy hunger."

People who have engaged in Zen study do not have clear minds; though there are many people who engage in Zen study, that doesn't matter. The states of mind of people engaged in Zen study are all bad. The way to clarify this one mind emerges from profound effort.

Takuan's opinion of contemporary Zen might be attributed to the fact that he died before the peak of the Zen revival, but the masters of the revival also spoke critically of the state of Zen students and schools of their time. The capture of Zen schools by patronage and politics, combined with the systems of caste and primogeniture, populated Buddhist establishments with people uninterested in enlightenment.

Where to Set the Mind

Where to set the mind? If you set your mind on an opponent's physical actions, your mind is taken up by the opponent's physical actions. If you set your mind on an opponent's sword, your mind is taken up by the opponent's sword. If you set your mind on the intent to kill an opponent, your mind is taken up by the intent to kill the opponent. If you set your mind on your own sword, your mind is taken up by your sword. If you set your mind on the determination not to get killed, your mind is taken up by the intention not to get killed. If you set your mind on the other's stance, your mind is taken up by the other's stance. The point is that there is nowhere at all to set the mind.

Zen master Xuansha explained the mental poise of the free mind in terms of avoiding the specific drawbacks of fixation, whether concrete or abstract: "If you stir, you produce the root of birth and death; if you're still, you get drunk in the village of oblivion. If stirring and stillness are both erased, you fall into empty annihilation; if stirring and stillness are both withdrawn, you presume upon buddha-nature. Be like a dead tree or cold ashes in the face of objects and situations, while acting responsively according to the time, without losing proper balance. A mirror reflects a multitude of images without their confusing its brilliance."

Some ask, "If we let our mind go outside of ourselves at all, that fixates the mind on its object, resulting in defeat by the opponent. So we should keep the mind down below the navel, not letting it go elsewhere, then adapt to the actions of the opponent." Of course, that may be so, but from the point of view of the transcendental level of Buddhism, to keep the mind below the navel and not let it go elsewhere is on a low level, nothing transcendental; it belongs to the phase of developmental practice, the stage of practicing respectfulness. It is the stage referred to by the exhortation of Mencius to "Seek the free mind." This is not the higher transcendental level; it is the state of mind labeled respectful.

Keeping the mind below the navel is commonly associated with sitting meditation in modern Zen sects, but it is extremely rare in traditional Zen instructions. It is originally a fragment of a more complete system of energy circulation used in Taoism and esoteric Buddhism. Its mention here in the seventeenth century seems to reflect the adaptation of Zen to Bushido that took place in the middle ages; the establishment of the practice in pure Zen circles occurred a little later through the influence of the Kokurin school following Hakuin. In the latter case, the practice was introduced as a healing technique from Taoism, after Hakuin wrote of having recovered from a complete mental and physical breakdown through the use of this method. Eventually it was popularized as a standard element of sitting meditation, but it has limitations and negative side effects. These are seldom recognized in Zen—the present text is a rare exception—but widely warned of in Taoist writings.

As for the free mind, I'll write about that in another letter for your perusal.

If you keep your mind below your navel, trying to keep it from going elsewhere, your mind will be taken up by the thought of not letting it go elsewhere; the initiative to act will be missing, and you'll become exceptionally inhibited.

According to Taoist writers, excessive persistence in this exercise also inhibits internal activities, such as blood circulation, ultimately resulting in adverse effects on the body.

Some people ask, "If we are inhibited and unable to act effectively even if we keep our mind unmoving under the navel, then where in our bodies should we set the mind?"

If you set your mind in your right hand, it will be taken up by your right hand and your physical action will be defective. If you set your mind in your eyes, your mind will be taken up by your eyes and your physical action will be defective. If you set your mind on your right foot, your mind will be taken up by your right foot and your physical action will be defective. If you set your mind on any one place, wherever it may be, the activity of other parts will be defective.

So, where should one set the mind? I reply that when you don't set it anywhere, it pervades your whole body, suffusing your whole being, so when it goes into your hands, it accomplishes the function of the hands, when it enters the feet, it accomplishes the function of the feet, when it enters the eyes, it accomplishes the function of the eyes. As it suffuses wherever it enters, it accomplishes the functions of wherever it enters. If you fix one place to set the mind, it will be taken up by that one place, so functioning will be defective.

> The original system containing concentration below the navel within it is for the purpose of circulation of conscious energy throughout the body. This is considered a contrived method, however, and many Taoists have abandoned it in favor of the so-called uncontrived method through which energy spontaneously fills the whole body. It is this latter spontaneous method that Zen master Takuan recommends.

When you think, it is taken up by thinking, so you should let your mind pervade your whole body without any more thought or discrimination, so that it is everywhere without being fixated anywhere, effectively accomplishing the functions proper to every part. That is to say that if you set your mind on one place you will become unbalanced. Being unbalanced means being lopsided. Balance is a matter of total pervasion; a balanced mind pervades the whole body with awareness, not sticking to one locus. Keeping your mind in one place while defective elsewhere is called having an unbalanced mind. Imbalance is undesirable.

This practical principle is illustrated in a famous Zen koan from the classic Blue Cliff Record *utilizing the image of Kannon of the Thousand Hands, which Zen master Takuan introduced earlier.*

In the Blue Cliff Record *story, Younger Brother asks Older Brother, "What does the Bodhisattva of Great Compassion do with so many hands and eyes?"*

Older Brother: "Like someone reaching back for the pillow at night."

Younger Brother: "I understand."

Older Brother: "How do you understand?"

Younger Brother: "All over the body are hands and eyes."

Older Brother: "You've said quite a bit, but that's only eighty percent."

Younger Brother: "What do you say?"

Older Brother: "Throughout the body are hands and eyes."

In this story, the act of reaching back for the pillow at night represents situational use of capacities represented by the thousand hands and eyes of compassion. The image of hands and eyes all over the body represents the perceptive dimension of attainment; the image of hands and eyes throughout the body represents the energetic dimension of attainment. In the stage of complete mastery, energy is imbued with perception, and perception is imbued with energy; this is the level of attainment to which Zen master Takuan alludes by his emphasis on balance.

In all things, inflexibility results in imbalance, so it is undesirable on the Way. If you don't think about where to set the mind, then the mind extends throughout the whole body, pervading it. It might be said that you should apply the mind to each situation according to the action of the opponent, without setting your mind on any particular point. Since it pervades the whole body, when you need your hands, you should use the mind in your hands; when you need your feet, you should use the mind in your feet. If you set it in one fixed place, then as you try to withdraw it from where you've set it in order to use it elsewhere, it halts there and so its function is defective.

If you try to keep your mind like a tethered cat, determined not to let it go anywhere else, keeping it on your own body, then the mind is taken up by your body. If you leave it be inside your body, it won't go anywhere else.

Effort to avoid halting in one place is all practice. Not letting the mind come to a halt anywhere is the eye, the essential point. If you don't set it anywhere, then it is everywhere. When you use your mind externally too, if you set the mind in one direction it will be missing in the other nine directions. If you don't set the mind in one direction, then the mind is in the ten directions!

The prototype of this teaching is in the Zen classic Record of Linji, Rinzai-roku *in Japanese. This, along with the* Blue Cliff Record, *was one of the main texts of the Rinzai school of Zen to which Takuan belonged. According to the classic, Zen master Linji said, "The reality of mind has no form but pervades the ten directions. In the eyes it is called seeing, in the ears it is called hearing, in the nose it smells, in the mouth it speaks, in the hands it grips, in the feet it steps. Basically it is a single spiritual light, differentiated into a sixfold combination. Once the whole mind is as nothing, you are liberated wherever you are." Also, in a similar vein, the teaching illustrates the practice: "The immediate solitary light clearly listening is unobstructed everywhere, pervading the ten directions, free in all realms, entering into the differentiations in objects without being changed." In the martial arts, this practice is applied to attainment of the ability to respond to events spontaneously as they arise, without getting trapped or thrown off balance anywhere, mentally, energetically, or physically.*

The Basic Mind and the Errant Mind

The basic mind is the mind that does not stay in a particular place but pervades the whole body and whole being. The errant mind is the mind that congeals in one place brooding about something; so when the basic mind congeals, focused on one point, it becomes the so-called errant mind.

When the basic mind is lost, its function is missing here and there, so the very effort not to lose it is the basic mind.

To make an analogy, the basic mind is like water that does not stagnate anywhere, while the errant mind is like ice that cannot be used for washing your hands or your head. When you melt ice into water so that it flows freely, then you can use it to wash your hands or feet or anything else.

When your mind congeals in one place, resting on one thing, it is like ice that cannot be used freely because it is solid—you can't wash your hands and feet with ice. Melting the mind to use it throughout the body like water, you can apply it wherever you wish. This is called the basic mind.

In terms of pure Zen, when the mind is trained to focus exclusively on specific objects and habituated to operating only in preconceived patterns, these objects and patterns become prisons of potential. Applied to the context of martial arts, this means that when the mind is frozen by fixation, instinctive response is inhibited. This causes energy to stagnate, so that it cannot be accessed freely and released instantly.

The Minding Mind and the Unminding Mind

The so-called minding mind is the same thing as the errant mind. The minding mind keeps thinking about something in particular, whatever it may be. When there is something on your mind, conceptual thought arises, so it is called the minding mind.

The unminding mind is the same thing as the aforementioned basic mind; it is the mind without any stiffness or fixation, the mind as it is without any conceptualization or thought. The mind that pervades the whole body and suffuses the whole being is called the unminding mind. It is the mind not set anywhere. It is not like stone or wood—not lingering anywhere is called unminding.

When it lingers, there is something on the mind; when it doesn't linger anywhere, there is nothing on the mind. Having nothing in mind is called the unminding mind; it is also called having no mind and no thoughts. When this unminding has effectively become mind, it does not stay on anything and does not miss anything. Like a channel filled with water, it is in the body and comes out when there is a need. The mind that fixates somewhere and lingers does not work freely.

A wheel turns because it is not fixed. If it were stuck in one place, it wouldn't turn. The mind too does not work when it is fixated in one place. If there is something on your mind you are thinking about, you can't hear what people say even if you are listening to them talk. That is because your mind is fixated on what you are thinking about.

With your mind on whatever you are thinking about, it inclines in one direction; when it inclines in one direction, you don't hear things even though you listen, and you don't see even when you look. This is because there is something on your mind. Having something on your mind means there is something you are thinking about. If you get rid of that thing on your mind, then the mind is unminding and only works when there is a need, fulfilling that need.

The idea of getting rid of whatever is on your mind also becomes something your mind. If you don't think about it, it disappears of itself, and you naturally become unminding. Persist in this, and before you realize it you will sponta-neously become that way; if you try to accomplish it in a hurry, you won't get there. An ancient verse says, "Intending not to think is still thinking of something; do you intend not to think you won't think?"

> One of the oldest Zen classics, Song of the Trusting Heart, *says, "If you stop movement to return to stillness, stopping makes even more movement: as long as you remain in dual extremes, how can you know they're of one kind? If you don't know they're of one kind, you'll lose efficacy in both domains."*

> The classic Rinzai-roku *says, "The ground of mind can enter into the ordinary and the sacred, the pure and the*

polluted, the absolute and the conventional, without being absolute or conventional, ordinary or sacred, yet able to give names to all that is absolute, conventional, ordinary, or sacred. One who has realized this cannot be labeled by the absolute or the conventional, by the ordinary or the sacred. If you can grasp it, then use it, without labeling it any more. This is called the mystic teaching."

In the context of martial arts, to be unminding, or having nothing on one's mind, is critical to liberation of both attention and energy from fixation and distraction to immediacy, openness, and fluidity.

Tossing a Gourd on Water—Push It Down and It Turns Over

If you toss a gourd on water and press on it, it bobs away—whatever you do, it won't stay in one place. The mind of a realized person does not rest on anything at all—it is like pushing down a gourd on the water.

The classical Zen master Yantou coined this image of Zen experience in action:

"This is like a gourd floating on water—can anyone keep it down? It is ever-present, flowing ceaselessly, independent and free—there has never been any doctrine that could encompass it, never any doctrine that could be its equivalent. It immediately appears on stimulus, turns freely on contact, encompassing sound and form. In extension it flows everywhere, without inhibition, always manifest before the eyes. How could this be a state of immobility? Go out, and nothing is not it; go in, and everything returns to the source."

Activate the Mind without Dwelling Anywhere

Whatever you do, if the thought of doing it arises, the mind rests on the thing to do. That being so, the point of this saying is to activate the mind without coming to a halt anywhere. If the mind is not activated where it is to be activated, action isn't initiated; if it is, the mind halts there. Activating the mind to do a task without halting is expertise in all fields.

The instruction to "activate the mind without dwelling anywhere" comes from the Diamond Cutter Scripture, *as mentioned before. This text was commonly recited in Japanese Zen schools. A commentary attributed to Huineng, the sixth grand master of Zen, says:*

"When your intrinsic nature always produces insightful wisdom, you act with an impartial, kind, and compassionate mind, and respect all people; this is the pure mind of a practitioner. If you do not purify your own mind but get obsessed with a pure state, your mind dwells on something—this is attachment to an image of a phenomenon. If you fixate on forms when you see forms, and activate your mind dwelling on form, then you are a deluded person. If you are detached from forms even as you see forms, and activate the mind without dwelling on forms, then you are an enlightened person. When you activate the mind dwelling on forms, it is like clouds covering the sky; when you activate the mind without dwelling on forms, then you are an enlightened person."

A clinging state of mind arises from that halting mind; routine habit too comes from there, so this halting mind becomes the yoke of life and death. Seeing the flowers and foliage, even as the mind seeing the flowers and foliage is activated, it does not halt there—that's the point. A poem by Ji-en says, "Fragrant as flowers at the brushwood door may be, I have already seen it—what a disappointing world!" In other words, "whereas the flowers are fragrant without minding, the world I have observed with my mind on the flowers and the mindfulness of myself having been affected by it are disappointing."

The poem by Ji-en (1155–1225), a high priest of the Tendai sect of Buddhism, evokes the Four-Part contemplation of Buddhist Yoga, in which experience is observed in four parts—the perceiver, the perceived, the self-witness, and the witness of the self-witness. This is used as a framework of introspective exercise to examine the relationship between objectivity and subjectivity and the internal contradictions in consciousness.

This means that in seeing and hearing, not fixating the mind on one point is considered the ultimate attainment. To the extent that respectful means focusing on one point without wandering off, you set your mind on one point and don't let it go anywhere else; even if you subsequently withdraw and cut it off, not letting the mind go to the cutting off is the essential thing.

As noted earlier, "respectfulness," or "seriousness," are neo-Confucian terms used as an equivalent of the Buddhist exercise of focusing the mind on one point. Because this is a preliminary exercise, and keeping the mind on one point inhibits free function, in Zen and martial arts it is essential to get beyond this stage. Even so, if the mind is then focused on cutting off one-pointed focus, that intent and effort also trap the mind. Thus the Zen master says it is essential not to let the mind fixate on cutting off.

Respect is particularly essential in the context of following directions, such as from a leader or superior. There is such a thing as respect in Buddhism too. We refer to ringing the bell of respectful announcement, where we ring a bell three times, join our palms, and speak respectfully. Intoning the name of Buddha first is this attitude of respectful speech; "focusing on one thing without wandering off" and "single-minded without being distracted" have the same meaning.

The neo-Confucian schools developed in Song Dynasty China in response to the overwhelming influence of Zen were imported to Japan in the middle ages, but did not assume intellectual orthodoxy until the final feudal period, which lasted from the early seventeenth until the mid-nineteenth centuries. All of the original founders of the Noumenal school of Confucianism in China studied with Zen masters, and their teachings are heavily influenced by Zen. In Japan, this variety of neo-Confucianism was imbedded within the intellectual element of Zen Buddhism until the seventeenth century, when it was laicized and it assumed independent status in the ideological and educational structure of the Japanese state.

Even so, in Buddhism the attitude of respect is not the ultimate goal; it is a method of practical learning to stabilize the mind and not let it be scattered. When you have practiced this for a long time, your mind goes freely wherever you send it. The aforementioned stage where you "activate the mind without dwelling anywhere" is the transcendental goal. The attitude of respect is the stage where you keep the mind from going anywhere else, assuming it will scatter if you let it, relentlessly keeping the mind under control. This is just a temporary task of keeping the mind from scattering; if you go on like this all the time, you become inhibited.

One of the hallmarks of original Zen is distinguishing means and end, relinquishing the means when the end is reached. This is also rooted in the teachings of the Diamond Cutter Scripture: *"You should not grasp the teaching, and should not grasp anything contrary to the teaching. In this sense the Buddha always says you know that Buddha's teaching is like a raft—even the teaching is to be abandoned, let alone what is contrary to the teaching."*

Suppose, for example, that you have a captive bird; as long as you have to keep your cat on a leash, it isn't tame. If you keep your mind inhibited like a cat on a leash, you won't be able to function as you wish. If you first train the cat so that it can live together with the bird and not hunt it even if you let it free to go wherever it wants, that is the sense of activating the mind without dwelling on anything. It is a matter of letting your mind go as you would free the cat, employing the mind in such a way that even if it goes wherever it wants the mind does not halt.

The influential Zen master Dahui wrote against crude inhibitory methods of mind training, explaining that trying to suppress thought to keep the mind still and quiet is like placing a rock on grass; once the rock is lifted, the grass regrows.

Speaking in terms of your martial art, kill without keeping your mind on your hands gripping your sword, striking forgetful of all strokes, and not setting your mind on the person. Realizing that the other person is void, your self is void too, and the hand that strikes and the sword that strikes are both empty as well, you shouldn't have your attention taken by the void!

This Zen pivot is illustrated in a famous koan registered in the classic Book of Serenity: *a seeker asked a master, "When not a single thing is brought, then what?" The master said, "Put it down." The seeker asked, "If I don't bring even a single thing, what should I put down?" The master said, "Then carry it out."*

When Zen Master Mugaku of Kamakura was captured by the Mongols in China and about to be put to death, he composed a verse ending with the words "in a lightning flash it cuts the spring breeze." Thereupon, they say, the soldier threw down his sword and ran away.

What Mugaku meant was the sword was upraised in a flash, like lightning; and in that lightning flash there is no mind, no thought at all—the striking sword has no mind, the killing man has no mind, and the self being killed has no mind. The killer is void, the sword is void, and the self that is killed is void—so the attacker is not a person, the striking sword is not a sword, and as far as the self being killed is concerned, it is like cutting in a flash through the wind blowing in the spring sky.

This is the mind that doesn't stay anywhere at all. The sword certainly is not aware of cutting through the wind!

Zen Master Mugaku (Wuxue 1226–1286) was a Chinese monk invited to Japan in 1280 by Hojo Tokimune, the eighth regent of the Kamakura Shogunate. Tokimune was responsible for dismissing the ambassador of the Mongol Khan, who responded by launching a fleet to invade Japan. Mugaku was appointed Founder of the still famous Engakuji monastery in Kamakura, the headquarters of the first military government of Japan.

Mugaku is said to have experienced his first Zen awakening at the age of twelve, when he overheard a monk reciting the lines, "Bamboo shadows sweep the stairs without any dust being stirred; moonlight penetrates the depths of the pond without leaving traces in the water." These phrases represent the Mahayana Buddhist ideal of transcending the world in its very midst. In the context of martial arts, this means maintaining coolness, detachment, presence of mind, and objectivity, even in the heat of combat.

The story of Mugaku's feat of "winning without fighting" is also cited to illustrate this ideal capacity of calm in the midst of a storm. Having fled invading Mongol armies in 1275, Mugaku was finally surrounded by advancing Mongol troops the next year. According to the story, he alone remained in the monastery where he had been staying, sitting in the communal hall, when all the other monks had disappeared. Threatened with a sword to his neck, the Zen master showed no sign of fear; instead, he extemporized,

"There's no place in the universe for a solitary walking stick;

Happily, I've found personality is void, and so are things.

Greetings to the Mongolian sword—

In a lightning flash it cuts the spring breeze."

The Mongol warriors were so impressed, it is said, that they apologized and left.

It is also said that Mugaku predicted the Mongolian invasion of Japan, but assured Tokimune that it would be unsuccessful. While extrasensory capacities are sometimes admitted of Zen masters, these predictions, which proved accurate, could have also been derived from knowledge of conditions on the continent and over the Sea of Japan, knowledge that had been accumulating for several generations among the Zen pilgrims traveling between Japan and China.

Expertise is doing everything entirely forgetful of your mind this way. When you dance, you brandish a fan as you step; if you conceive the intention to move your hands and feet skillfully to dance well, unable to forget it entirely, you cannot be called expert. As long as your mind is fixed on your hands and feet, the performance won't be entertaining. Everything you do without complete abandonment of mind is lousy.

Like Zen archery, as noted earlier, the underlying "unminding" principle of Zen and the ways has its direct Taoist precursor in a story found in the classic Liezi:

"Zhao Xiangzi led a party of a hundred thousand hunting in Zhongshan, trampling the growth, burning the woods, fanning the flames for miles. A man emerged from a rock wall and bobbed up and down with the smoke. Everyone thought it was an apparition. Then when the fire had passed, he ambled out as if he hadn't been through anything at all.

"Xiangzi thought this strange, and kept him for observation. His form and features were those of a human,

his breathing and his voice were those of a human. 'How did you stay inside the rock?' he asked; 'How did you go into the fire?'

"That man said, 'What is it you are calling "rock"? What is it you are calling "fire"?'

"Xiangzi said, 'What you just came out of is rock; what you just walked on was fire.'

"The man said, 'I didn't know.'

"When the Marquis Wen of Wei heard about this, he asked Zixia, 'What kind of man is that?'

"Zixia said, 'According to what I heard from Confucius, harmony means universal assimilation to things; then things cannot cause injury or obstruction, and it is possible even to go through metal and stone, and walk on water and fire.'

"Marquis Wen said, 'Why don't you do it?'

"Zixia said, 'I am as yet unable to clear my mind of intellection. Even so, I have time to try to talk about it.'

"Marquis Wen asked, 'Why didn't Confucius do it?'

"Zixia said, 'Confucius was one of those who was able to do it yet was able to not do it.'

"Marquis Wen was delighted."

Don't Let the Mind Go

This is a saying of the philosopher Mencius. The idea is to find the mind gone astray and return it to oneself. The point is that the mind is the master of the body, but when the mind has run off into unwholesome paths, why not find it and bring it back, just as one might go find a dog, cat, or hen that has wandered away and bring it back home.

Of course, this is the obvious meaning. Nevertheless, the scholar Shao Kangjie said, "The mind should be released," changing it right around. The idea expressed here is that if you keep the mind confined you get tired and, like a cat, you can't function; so let your mind go, using it skillfully in such a way as not to fixate mentally on things and not be affected by them.

When the mind is affected by and fixated on things, and it is therefore said to avoid being affected or fixated, to return the mind to oneself, that is the stage of beginners' practice. Be like a lotus unstained by the mud—being in the mud doesn't matter. Make your mind like a highly polished crystal that isn't affected even in the mud, letting it go wherever it will. If you restrain your mind, you'll be inhibited. You may control your mind, but that's a task for the beginner, you know. If you spend your whole life on that, you'll never reach the higher stage but wind up at a lower stage.

During the phase of practicing, it is good to keep the attitude of not letting the mind go, as Mencius said. When you reach the consummation, it is as Shao Kangjie said—the mind must be released.

There is an expression "see the released mind" in the sayings of Chan Master Zhongfeng. This means the same thing as Shao Kangjie's "the mind must be released." It means that you should seek the freed mind and not keep it on one point.

The expression "fully unregressing" is also from Zhongfeng. It means keeping the mind unchanging without regression. It means that even if people succeed once or twice, they should still continue to maintain a mind that eventually never regresses.

Mencius (372–289 BCE) was a Confucian scholar, but parts of his work were also valued by Taoists and Buddhists. In Japan, the book of Mencius was one of four Confucian classics constituting a common primary curriculum. Shao Kangjie (1011–1077), an expert in the I Ching, *was one of the founding scholars of the neo-Confucian movement of Song Dynasty China, which was highly influenced by Zen and known as noumenalism, idealism, or the study of inner design. Zhongfeng (1263–1323) was one of the last distinguished Zen masters of China to become known in Japan. His teaching emphasizes intense concentration, particularly with the use of sayings or phrases such as noted here in Takuan's treatment of meditation in a Zen-Confucian mode.*

Tossing a Ball on the Water, Not Stopping Moment to Moment

If you throw a ball onto a rushing stream, it will ride the waves unstopping.

This image comes from the Zen classic The Blue Cliff Record: *A student asked a teacher, "Does a newborn infant also have six consciousnesses?" The teacher said, "A ball tossed on rushing water." The student asked another teacher the meaning of tossing a ball on swiftly flowing water; the teacher said, "Moment-to-moment nonstop flow." The term "six consciousnesses" refers to the elementary sense consciousnesses—seeing, hearing, and so on—plus cognitive consciousness. Some commentators read "sixth consciousness," which refers specifically to cognitive consciousness. A verse on this anecdote says, "A ball tossed on boundless rushing water—it doesn't stay where it lands; who can watch?" The newborn baby stands for presence of mind in the moment, referred to in Zen terminology as "mirror-like consciousness." A prose comment explains, "The moment is fleeting as a lightning flash." In the context of martial arts, this ongoing presence of mind is the basis of instantaneous perception and reaction in the midst of rapid and unpredictable change.*

Before and After Cut Off

If you don't give up a previous state of mind and also leave a present state of mind for the future, that is bad. The idea here is to sever the past from the present. This is called cutting off the connection between before and after. It means not stopping the mind.

"Cutting off the connection between before and after" is a technical expression for the basic Zen experience of presence in the moment. When attention lingers on what has already past or carries what it clings to into the future, awareness of the ongoing present is compromised by this artificial continuity. In energetic terms, when attention is pulled into the past or pushed into the future, energy is drained by tension in the gap between awareness and immediate actuality. Therefore in martial arts the connection between past and present is broken to keep freeing attention and energy in the ongoing present.

Advice to Yagyu Munenori

I understand you seek my critical advice on matters of concern to you. I don't know how you will like my ideas, but I will take the chance to write you so you might read them.

You are a master of martial arts without equal in the past or the present. Because of this your official rank, your salary, and your reputation are all excellent. You should think only of gratitude and loyalty day and night, never even dreaming of forgetting this immense favor.

Loyalty means first of all balancing your own mind and governing yourself, having no duplicity in your relation to your ruler, not being resentful or blaming others, going to work every day diligently, being filial to your parents at home, being faithful in marriage, observing proper courtesies and duties, not falling in love with concubines, giving up addiction to sex, acting properly with dignity in the company of parents, not separating yourself from employees by personal interests, employing good people and allowing them access to you so they can point out where you have fallen short, administering national policy correctly, keeping corrupt people away—when you act thus, good people advance day by day, while corrupt people are spontaneously reformed by their employer's desire for good.

When rulers and ministers, superiors and subordinates are thus good people, not greedy or extravagant, the country waxes wealthy, the people have plenty and are content, and children are close to their parents, the country will naturally be peaceful. This is the beginning of loyalty.

When you employ seasoned and loyal warriors like this for official occasions and duties, you can direct even a thousand or ten thousand men at will. Just as the thousand hands of Kannon are all useful as long as the mind is balanced, as mentioned before, if the heart of your martial art is balanced, the activity of your mind is free, as if you could subdue thousands of enemies with one sword. Is this not great loyalty?

When the mind is balanced, it is not something others know from outside. Good and bad both come from the emergence of thought. If you think about the root of good and bad, and do good while refraining from bad, your heart will naturally be honest. If you know something is bad yet don't stop it, that is because there is something wrong with your predilections.

For example, you may like sex, but are you going to make it into an overindulgent obsession? When some sort of predilection works on your mind, even if there are good people you won't like them and won't employ their good offices. Even if people are ignoramuses, on the other hand, once you like them you'll promote them; so even if there are good people, as long as you don't employ them it's as if there were no good people at all. Then no matter how many thousands of people are available, there will be no one of use to the leadership when the time comes.

The corrupt among the ignorant youths who have come into favor for a time have always had perverted minds, so they have never entertained a single thought of sacrificing their lives in an emergency. I have never heard of anyone in history whose mind is corrupt doing any good for his government. I am very distressed by reports that this kind of thing is also happening in your setting up your disciples. All of them are infected by this illness on account of a bit of luck, not knowing that they're falling into evil. They may think no one knows, denying that the subtle will come to light, but if they know it in their own hearts, then heaven, earth, ghosts, spirits, and the people all know it. Isn't this a dangerous way to defend the country? That's why I think it is serious disloyalty.

For example, no matter how ardently you yourself want to be loyal to the leadership, if the members of the whole family are not in harmony, and the people of Yagyu Valley Village rebel, everything will go awry.

They say that if you want to know people's merits and faults, you can tell by the help they employ and the friends with whom they associate. If the leader is good, the members of the cabinet are all good people. If the leader is not right, his cabinet and friends are all wrong. Then they disregard the populace and look down on other countries.

This is what is meant by the saying that people will feel friendly toward you if you are good. It is said that a country should consider good people a treasure. Recognizing this sincerely, if you get rid of subjective injustice in your knowledge of others, making it a priority to avoid petty people and take to the wise, the government of the country will improve and you can be the most loyal of ministers.

Regarding the behavior of your son, in particular, if the parent's own conduct is not correct, it is contradictory to censure the wrongdoing of the child. Straighten yourself first, and then if there is any further controversy, be correct yourself and your younger son will also straighten out by following the example of his older brother. Then father and sons will all be good. That will be auspicious.

It is said that taking and leaving should be done justly. Now that you are a favored member of the cabinet, you should never accept bribes from the warlords, forgetting justice for greed.

You like to dance, and take pride in your ability. You are pressed to come forward before the assembly of warlords and urged to dance. I think this is completely unhealthy. I hear you say the shogun's singing is like the monkey music of farcical drama. And I hear you intercede strongly with the shogun on behalf of warlords who treat you well. Shouldn't you think this over carefully? A poem says, "Since it is the mind that misleads the mind, don't leave the mind to the mind."

Takuan was known for fearlessness in his dealings with worldly powers, and this is reflected in his forthright advice to Yagyu Munenori, who was by then sword master to the shogun and chief of the shogun's secret police. Takuan was the Zen teacher of an emperor, shogun, and a number of feudal lords, but he also refused the patronage of certain powerful warlords and retired from the abbacy of the highest ranked Zen monastery in Japan just three days after his debut. After the military government imposed its own regulations on the Zen orders, Takuan was sent into exile for four years for criticizing these rules as inconsistent with the reality of Zen.

TAI-A KI: NOTES ON THE PEERLESS SWORD

By Zen Master Takuan (1573–1645)

It seems that the art of war is not a contest for supremacy, and not a matter of relative strength. Not taking a step forward, not taking a step backward, I am not seen by opponents, I do not see opposition. Penetrating the place where heaven and earth have not divided and yin and yang do not reach, directness will attain success.

"I am not seen by opponents" refers to the true self, not to self in contrast to others. The self in contrast to others is visible to people, but people seldom see the true self. That is why "I am not seen by opponents."

"I do not see opposition" means having no notion of self in contrast to others, so one does not see the martial art of an opponent's personal self. But not seeing opposition does not mean that one does not see the opponent before one's eyes; subtlety is to see without seeing.

The true self is the self that is prior to the division of heaven and earth, before your parents conceived and gave birth. This self is the self that is in all animate things, birds and beasts, grasses and trees. This is what is called buddha-nature.

Therefore this self is self that has no shadow or form, no birth or death. It is not the self that is seen by the present physical eye. Only enlightened people can see it. Those who have seen it are called people who have seen nature and realized buddhahood.

In ancient times the Buddha went into the Himalaya mountains and attained enlightenment after six years of hardship. This was awakening to the true self. This is not something that ordinary people with no power of faith can realize in three to five years.

People studying the path spend ten to twenty years faithfully calling on teachers, without slacking off at all, undeterred by hardship and toil, like parents who've lost their children, never retreating from their determination, pondering profoundly, seeking intently, finally to reach the point where even notions of Buddha and Dharma are all gone; then they spontaneously see this.

"Penetrating the place where heaven and earth have not divided and yin and yang do not reach, directness will attain success" means to focus on the point where heaven and earth are as yet undivided, where neither dark nor light reach, and see directly without constructing opinions or interpretations; then you will have great success.

This introductory passage illustrates essential tactics on two levels. Externally, it presents the appearance of a philosophical or metaphysical front, which conceals a hidden maneuver; as such, it is an illustration of the essential design of tactical deception. On the inward plane, the passage contains directions to a state of inaccessibility essential to both Zen and martial arts. Removing fixation of attention from the person frees it for sensing of energetic movement, thus enabling the martial artist to respond to opponents' moves more fluidly and spontaneously than possible through the medium of cognitive consciousness. In energetic terms, this implies retrieving energy from attachment and dissipation in objects conceived as such, be it an opponent, oneself, or weapons, maintaining awareness of these things in the mirroring state of immediate open awareness rather than discrete units of attention. Energy thus conserved is then sunk into a subliminal sense deep inside the energetic body, where it can detect external pressures without being tapped and drained.

Adepts do not use the sword to kill people; they use the sword to let people live. When it is necessary to kill, they kill; when it is necessary to let live, they let live. Killing is the *samadhi* of killing, letting live is the *samadhi* of letting live. They can see right and wrong without seeing right and wrong; they can discriminate without discriminating. They walk on water as on land, walk on land as on water. Whoever attains this freedom is invincible against anyone on earth and is utterly peerless.

The moral basis of the science of martial arts is derived from Taoism. The Te-Tao Ching *says, "Good warriors are not militaristic, good fighters don't get angry, and those who are good at defeating opponents don't get caught up in it." The same classic says, "If you go into battle with kindness, then you will prevail; if you use it for defense, then you will be secure."*

When the moral quality of a conflict is clear, then energy can be freely released into action without reservation or hesitation. This is the meaning of the word "samadhi," a Sanskrit term borrowed from Buddhist meditation science meaning absorption. In this sense, absorption implies unification of subject and object, or perhaps more properly speaking, elimination of gaps and barriers between subject and object. In the context of martial arts, this is what enables energetic sensing to respond to external states and movements without being depleted or diffused by contact or impact.

Adepts refers to people adept at martial arts. Not using a sword to kill people means that even though you don't kill people with a sword, people all spontaneously shrink back on encountering this principle and become dead folks, so there's no need to kill anyone.

Letting people live means that while you use a sword to deal with people, you let opponents do what they will, just being yourself, with the attitude of a spectator.

Killing is the samadhi of killing, letting live is the samadhi of letting live—this means that whether you let live or kill is entirely up to you.

Being able to see right and wrong without seeing right and wrong, being able to discriminate without discriminating, means being able to see right and wrong without seeing right and wrong in the context of martial arts, able to discriminate without discriminating. For example, when a mirror is uncovered, it reflects the forms of whatever objects are in front of it, but the mirror itself is mindless, so even though it reflects objects accurately it does not have any intention of distinguishing one thing from another.

For a person using martial arts as well, when the mirror of the unified mind is uncovered, even though it has no intention of discriminating right and wrong, because the mirror of mind is clear, distinctions of right and wrong are visible without showing.

As for the meaning of walking on water as on land and walking on land as on water, this cannot be known by any but those who have realized the original source of humanity. If ignorant people tried to walk on water as on land, they'd even sink on land; if they tried to walk on land as on water, they'd think they could walk on water. Therefore this principle can only be reached, in fact, by people who have forgotten both land and water.

"Whoever attains this freedom is invincible against anyone on earth" means that if a martial artist has attained such freedom, even if everyone on earth got together to plot they couldn't do anything. *Peerless* means having no match in the world—"In the heavens above and on earth below, I alone am honored."

This concept of invincible freedom also has a precedent in the Taoist classic Liezi:

"Liezi asked Gatekeeper Yin, 'Complete people can travel underwater without obstruction, walk on fire without getting burnt, can go beyond all beings without fear. How do they get to be this way?'

"Gatekeeper Yin said, 'This is the protection of pure energy, not of a kind with cunning and cleverness, resolution and daring. Stay a while and I'll tell you.

"Whatever has appearance, form, sound, or color is a thing. How can things be so disparate? And which of them can take precedence, when they are only forms?

"Things are created in the formless and end in the unalterable. How can any who plumb this stop here? They live by measures without excess, take refuge in a beginningless order, roam where things end and begin. They unify their essence, nurture their energy, and store their power, to commune with the creation of things.

146

"When they are like this, their nature is kept whole, their spirit has no gaps — how can anything get access to them?

"When a drunken man falls from a cart, he may get hurt, but does not die. His bones and joints are the same as other people's, but his injury is different from others because his spirit is whole. He doesn't know when he's riding, and he doesn't know when he's falling either. Neither death nor life, surprise nor fear, enter into his chest, so he is not frightened when he encounters things.

" 'If even one who gains wholeness in wine is like this, how about one who gains wholeness in Nature? Sages take refuge in Nature, so things cannot harm them.' "

Do you want to attain this? Whether walking, standing, sitting, or reclining, speaking or silent, at tea and at meals, keep up unremitting effort, constantly focusing on finding out; you must see directly. Over months and years it will naturally be as if you found a lamp in the dark, attaining teacherless knowledge and exercising uncontrived action. At this time you transcend the ordinary without leaving the ordinary. This is called the *Tai-A*, the peerless sword.

"Keep up unremitting effort, constantly focusing on finding out; you must see directly" means that you always return to yourself and focus intently, investigating the principle without slacking off, right being right and wrong being wrong, simply and directly, seeing this principle in everything.

To attain teacherless knowledge means to realize the fundamental knowledge that even a teacher cannot convey. As for exercising uncontrived action, all actions of ordinary people come from consciousness, so they are all conditioned activities that are only misery; on the other hand, this uncontrived activity comes from fundamental knowledge, so it is simply natural and easy. Thus it is called subtle function.

Transcending the ordinary without leaving the ordinary means that this uncontrived subtle function is not activated in some special state, but is a matter of all everyday activities becoming uncontrived. So it is not a matter of departure from the ordinary. Nevertheless, it is completely different from the usual contrivances of ordinary people, even though it is not out of the ordinary it transcends the ordinary.

The Tai-A is the name of a sword that has no equal. This famous sword can cut through iron, even stone—nothing in the world can stop its blade. Someone who has attained the aforementioned uncontrived subtle function cannot be opposed by the top general of the armed forces, nor by a million powerful opponents, just as nothing can stand up to the Tai-A sword. Therefore the power of this subtle function is likened to the Tai-A sword.

> *"Teacherless knowledge," or fundamental knowledge, refers to firsthand experiential knowledge that is not learned or acquired, but rather to be uncovered and activated. The uncontrived function that emerges from this teacherless knowledge is spontaneous, acting on direct perception rather than constructed conception. Applied to martial arts, this fundamental knowledge and uncontrived function are associated with immediacy of sense and response in action.*

This sharp sword Tai-A is inherent in everyone, complete in each individual. Those who understand it are feared by celestial demons, while those who are ignorant of it are cheated by cultists. Sometimes experts' blades cross, with neither winner nor loser; when Buddha held up a flower, Kasyapa smiled. Even understanding three corners when one is brought up, judging grains and ounces at a glance, is ordinary keenness; those who have finished this task cut right into three before one is even brought up, before three are understood — how about face-to-face confrontation?

To say that this sharp sword Tai-A is inherent in everyone, complete in each individual, means there is nothing that can stand up to its blade. The famous Tai-A sword is not with another, but is inherent in everyone, with no lack at all, complete and perfect. This refers to the mind.

This mind is not born at birth and does not die at death, so it is called the original face. Even the sky cannot cover this, even the earth cannot support it; even fire cannot burn it, even water cannot wet it, even wind cannot penetrate it. Therefore there is nothing in the world that can resist its blade.

"Those who understand it are feared by celestial demons, while those who are ignorant of it are cheated by cultists" means that those who have realized this original face cannot be blocked by anything in the universe, so there is no way for celestial demons to work their magic. On the contrary, they are seen through completely, so they fear such a person and cannot approach. In contrast to this, those who are ignorant of this original face store up all sorts of deluded thoughts and false conceptions, and so, since they are obsessed by those deluded thoughts and false conceptions, cultists can easily deceive them.

"Sometimes experts' blades cross, with neither winner nor loser; when Buddha held up a flower, Kasyapa smiled." If people who have both realized the original face meet, and both draw the Tai-A sword, there is no way to determine the winner and loser in a contest—what then? The answer is that it is like the meeting of the Buddha and Kasyapa.

When Buddha held up a flower, Kasyapa smiled. At the last assembly on Spiritual Mountain, the Buddha held up a flower before a crowd of eighty thousand; all remained silent, except for Kasyapa, who smiled. Then the Buddha knew that Kasyapa had attained enlightenment, and testified, "I entrust to you the truth that is specially transmitted outside of doctrine, without literalism."

After that, this truth was transmitted through twenty-eight generations in India, to Bodhidharma; and in China, it was transmitted for six generations from Bodhidharma, to the Sixth Grand Master. This Zen master was a living bodhisattva, so Buddhism flourished in China after him, offshoots spreading, with five schools and seven sects emerging. In Japan, the bloodline has continued to the present day, from Xutang in China through his Japanese successor Daio and the latter's successor Daito.

Given this much, the teaching of holding up the flower and smiling is difficult to attain with certainty. It is not easy to know by speculation. Even the Buddhas gasp and fall silent at this. Though there is thus no way to express this principle in words, in a pinch it might be said that this is the point where the eyes of the Buddha and Kasyapa were one, like a bowl of water poured into another bowl, water and water merging without distinction. There is no more order of precedence.

Thus there isn't a single martial artist in a hundred thousand who has attained this teaching of holding up a flower and smiling, but if there is anyone on the Greatest Vehicle who wants to know, study for thirty more years! If you go wrong, not only will you fail to master martial arts, you will go to hell as fast as an arrow. Better watch out!

"Understanding three corners when one is brought up" and "judging grains and ounces at a glance" refer to people with sharp faculties and mental keenness. The point of saying that this is ordinary keenness is that for someone who is so sharp, being so keen all the time is nothing special. People who have realized the conditions of the great concern of Buddhism have already cut into three before one is even brought up, before three are understood, before any signs at all are evident, so nothing can be done when encountering someone like this. How much less in face-to-face confrontation—when someone who has attained the subtlety of speedy action like this, when he meets others, his skill is such that they are so easy to cut down they don't even realize their heads have fallen.

> *The Zen masters mentioned here are representatives of the lineage of "special transmission," which means mind-to-mind communication without words. The story of Buddha holding up a flower and his disciple Kasyapa smiling at the unspoken message is one of the key Zen stories used to illustrate this.*

> *"Understanding three corners when one is brought up" is a paraphrase of Confucius, who is reported to have said that if he brought up one corner of an issue to someone who couldn't come back with the other three, he wouldn't talk to that person any more. Zen texts often cite Confucius as a symbol of ordinary intellect; the saying that it is still ordinary to understand three corners when one is raised comes from the Zen classic* Blue Cliff Record.

"Cut into three" is another Zen expression, deriving from a meditation technique of the parent Tendai school, by which all things are apprehended as simultaneously empty, actual, and in between these extremes. By apprehending things as empty, the mind is freed of inhibition; by apprehending things as actual, the mind is kept from oblivion; by apprehending things as in between, the mind is able to perceive without fixation on perceptions.

Bodhidharma is considered the founder of Zen in China, in the sense of bringing this direct transmission outside of doctrine. In Taoism Bodhidharma is also associated with Shaolin boxing and so-called "sinew easing and marrow cleansing" meditation.

"The Sixth Grand Master of Zen" was Huineng, an illiterate woodcutter said to have realized teacherless knowledge. He was suddenly enlightened on hearing the line of the Diamond Cutter Scripture *that says, "Activate the mind without dwelling anywhere."*

Xutang (1185–1269) was one of the last distinguished Zen masters of the Song dynasty in China. He is particularly well known in Japanese tradition because he was the teacher of the pilgrim Daio (1235–1309), who introduced this line of Zen into Japan. Daito (1282–1338) was the principal Zen successor of Daio. This lineage was the most influential school of Rinzai Zen in Japanese history.

People like this never show their point; they are faster than lightning, quicker than a gale. Without such skills, after all, you'll hurt your hand on the point as you wield and brandish, falling short of expertise. Don't try to figure it out with conditioned consciousness; it cannot be conveyed by words, cannot be learned from models—this is the reality communicated outside of doctrine.

This real true martial art cannot be conveyed by words; there is no way to teach things like how to take up a stance and where to strike. Since it cannot be conveyed in words and cannot be taught by manners, it is called a specially transmitted reality outside of doctrine. To say that it is a reality specially transmitted outside of doctrine means that one must realize it and attain it oneself apart from a teacher's instruction.

When great function manifests, it does not keep to regulations; going in harmony, going in opposition, even the deities cannot fathom—what principle is this? An ancient said, "My home has no protective talisman—it isn't haunted." One who is cultivated enough to attain this principle can pacify the whole land with one sword. Those who study it should not slight it.

When the great function of that specially transmitted reality appears before your eyes, it is independent and free; it does not maintain regulations. However, this great function reaches everywhere in the universe; it is called great function because there is nowhere outside it. Regulations are rules and laws; rules and laws, which are like molds that form things, do not exist in the manifestation of the great function.

People in whom this great function is manifest are free to go along or against the current, without impediment. Even the deities cannot fathom it. What principle is this?—here's the challenge. "My home has no protective talisman—it isn't haunted" is the reply to this challenge. People whose house isn't haunted to begin with don't even think of putting up protective talismans.

The point of all this is that even the deities cannot read the minds of those who are able to use both harmony and opposition; escaping both pain and pleasure, as their bodies and minds are not haunted they have no inclination for talismans either—their state is splendidly clear.

Someone who is thoroughly cultivated, to the point of having attained liberation with sword in hand, will be like the founder of the Han dynasty, who pacified the continent with a single sword. Those who study these subtle principles of the sword should not entertain crude concepts, but make their minds highly concentrated, working intently, without slacking off at all.

REFERENCES

～

Texts Cited

The Art of War by Sun Tzu. Translated by Thomas Cleary. Boston: Shambhala, 1988.

The Art of Wealth. Translated by Thomas Cleary. Deerfield Beach, FL: Health Communications, 1998.

The Blue Cliff Record. Translated by Thomas Cleary and J. C. Cleary. Boston: Shambhala, 1992.

The Book of Serenity. Translated by Thomas Cleary. Boston: Shambhala, 1998.

The Diamond Cutter Scripture. In *The Sutra of Hui-neng, Grandmaster of Zen.* Translated by Thomas Cleary. Boston: Shambhala, 1998.

The Flower Ornament Scripture. Translated by Thomas Cleary. Boston, Shambhala, 1993.

Liezi. See Thomas Cleary, *Vitality, Energy, Spirit.* Boston: Shambhala, 1991.

Master of Demon Valley. In *Thunder in the Sky.* Translated by Thomas Cleary. Boston: Shambhala, 1993.

Master of the Hidden Storehouse. In *Thunder in the Sky.* Translated by Thomas Cleary. Boston: Shambhala, 1993.

Secrets of the Blue Cliff Record. Translated by Thomas Cleary. Boston: Shambhala, 2000.

Song of the Trusting Heart. In Thomas Cleary, *Instant Zen.* Berkeley: North Atlantic Books, 1994.

Tao Te Ching, In Thomas Cleary, *The Essential Tao.* San Francisco: Harper Collins, 1991.

Zen Masters Cited

Baizhang—see Thomas Cleary, *A Pocket Zen Reader*. Boston: Shambhala. 1999.

Bodhidharma—see *The Blue Cliff Record,* A Pocket Zen Reader; *Transmission of Light,* Translated by Thomas Cleary. San Francisco: North Point Press, 1990.

Bunan—see Thomas Cleary, *The Original Face*. New York: Grove Press, 1978.

Chinul—see Thomas Cleary, *Minding Mind.* Boston: Shambhala. 1995.

Dahui—see Thomas Cleary, *Zen Essence.* Boston: Shambhala. 1989.

Daito—see *The Original Face*.

Fayan—see Thomas Cleary, *The Five Houses of Zen*. Boston: Shambhala. 1998.

Foyan—see Thomas Cleary, *Instant Zen*. Berkeley: North Atlantic Press, 1994.

Hakuin—see Thomas Cleary, *Kensho, the Heart of Zen*. Boston: Shambhala, 1997.

Hui-neng—see *The Sutra of Hui-neng, Grand Master of Zen*. Translated by Thomas Cleary. Boston: Shambhala, 1998.

Kasyapa—see *Transmission of Light*.

Layman Pang—see *The Blue Cliff Record*.

Longji—see *The Book of Serenity*.

Man-an—see *Minding Mind*.

Manora—see *Transmission of Light*.

Mazu—see *The Five Houses of Zen*.

Xuansha—see *The Five Houses of Zen*.

Yantou—see *The Blue Cliff Record*.

Zhongfeng—see Thomas Cleary, *Teachings of Zen*. Boston: Shambhala, 1998.